Getting the
Best
Out of
Public Schools

Getting the Best Out of Public Schools

Dr. Steven & Virelle Kidder

FOREWORD BY DENNIS RAINEY

BROADMAN
& HOLMAN
PUBLISHERS

Nashville, Tennessee

0-8054-6374-7

Published by Broadman & Holman Publishers, Nashville, Tennessee
Page Design: Anderson Thomas Design
Acquisitions Editor: Vicki Crumpton
Page Composition: TF Designs

Dewey Decimal Classification: 370.11
Subject Heading: EDUCATION—PUBLIC SCHOOLS/EDUCATION—PARENT PARTICIPA-
TION—UNITED STATES/EDUCATIONAL CHANGE—UNITED STATES/CHURCH AND
EDUCATION—UNITED STATES
Library of Congress Card Catalog Number: 98-14155

Unless otherwise stated all Scripture citation is from the NIV, the Holy Bible, New International Version, copyright © 1973, 1978, 1984 by International Bible Society.

Library of Congress Cataloging-in-Publication Data
Kidder, Steven 1944–
      Getting the best out of public schools / Steven and Virelle Kidder.
         p.   cm.
      Includes bibliographical references.
      ISBN 0-8054-6374-7 (pbk.)
      1. Moral education—United States. 2. Public schools—United States. 3. Church and education—
United States. 4. Education—Parent participation—United States 5. Home and school—United
States. 6. Educational change—United States.   I. Kidder, Virelle. II. Title.
LC311.K53   1998
370.11'4'0973—dc21
                                                                                                      98-14155
                                                                                                      CIP

1 2 3 4 5 02 01 00 99 98

for Amy, our Champ

Contents

Foreword by Dennis Rainey

As parents of six children who have all spent time in public schools, Barbara and I believe in the public school choice for educating our children. That decision was not an easy one.

The bottom line is that we believe God led us not only to educate our children in public schools, but also to go to battle on behalf of the millions of children who are there as well. Public education is fraught with problems such as crime, godless philosophies, loss of focus on real educational instruction, and a frightening number of teachers and administrators who have lost heart. They have been overwhelmed by the emotional needs and character deficiencies of children who fill their classrooms.

In spite of all these problems, Barbara and I believe Christians can have a strategic place in public education. Across the country, we've found a surprising number of teachers and administrators who proudly bear the name of Christ and see their assignment as a mission to an unreached group of young people. We've seen how committed parents can make a real difference in the public school atmosphere. Our experience in public education has been one of our family's biggest challenges, but definitely one of the most rewarding.

I can still recall the first school I visited as a parent. I felt lost. It was unfamiliar territory. I didn't know the "lay of the land" or the "rules of the game." We wasted a lot of time finding out what was truly going on in our schools. I wish we had known Dr. Steven Kidder and his wife Virelle. Their experience in education would have saved us thousands of hours. *Getting the Best out of Public Schools* should become a well-worn volume in your home because it provides blueprints for building a positive public school experience for our children.

The Kidders give the public school parent the unvarnished truth about what they'll be facing in public schools. This is not a book of philosophical fluff, but a hard-hitting, practical battle plan that will equip you as a parent to love and lead your children through their public school experience.

The Kidders are committed to helping you make a difference. Filled with hope, their book will enable you to spot the dangers before they damage your child. It will show you how you can overhaul your school's educational goals, how you can become a mom or dad of influence and bring about change in the classroom or boardroom, and how you can bring "salt and light" into a very needy system. Every parent needs to digest the nourishment these pages provide. There is no doubt that the educational reformation needed in our nation must be led by Christian parents who know what is necessary and how to lead the change in the right direction.

May God's favor be upon you as a parent as you embark on one of the battlefields that Christians must win.

Dennis Rainey
Executive Director, FamilyLife

Acknowledgments

Writing this book was truly a test. First, it was a marriage test second only to wallpapering a bathroom together. Thanks to the fervent prayers of our family and friends, we not only survived; we actually enjoyed the experience, which has forever redefined *tolerance* and *grace* for us.

Second, it was an endurance test, as we learned to squeeze enormous amounts of communication and labor into many oddly spaced and inventive work periods. We have come to appreciate the African concept of the "rubber hour," having stretched many of them by now.

And last, this was a test of faith. Could God really take us through the new and, at times, frightening landscape of writing a book together during an equally frightening period of adversity of all sorts? (The devil dragged out his heavy artillery.) Yes, he could and he did. Therefore, we offer this book to him for his glory and honor and with the humblest of thanks. God is enough. He has proven it yet again to two grateful souls.

This book truly separated the sheep from the goats with our family and friends. Only the utterly faithful and patient survived. To those who prayed daily, listened to us whine, and waited forever to see us, we offer our deepest thanks. There are many more stars in your crown.

Our children have been an unending support and encouragement. Lauren and Michael, Amy, David, Bob and Theresa and little Logan—we thank you and love you! To our parents and other family cheerleaders—you have been wonderful!

Particular thanks go to many others who have made the way smoother, more joyful, even easy:

Ron Haynes, our agent, died suddenly during the revisions for this book. Ron was always a steady light, a cheerful voice, and radiated far more confidence in us than we had. We will miss him terribly.

Vicki Crumpton, our editor, is second to none. Working together on yet another book has been a terrific privilege and a great learning experience. Broadman & Holman knows how to make their authors feel very special.

To Dennis Rainey, who believed in the importance of this book before it was written and then agreed to write the Foreword: Thank you! We are honored.

Special thanks go to those who have given us the boost (or the shove!) we needed:

- Jim Dahlman at Focus on the Family for planting the seeds of thought that grew into this book,
- Chuck Johnson at Focus on the Family for providing much help and many resources,
- Kim Nelson at Family Life Ministries, who gave us great encouragement,
- Neil Boron, host of "Lifeline" on the Crawford Radio Network, not only for interviewing us so often, but also for being an all-around great friend and example,
- Gordon MacDonald for saying, "Get it written!"
- Eric Buehrer, Vernie Schorr, Tom Lickona, Lori Wiley, and others who are giants in the field of character education and schooling and yet took time to talk with us, send materials, and encourage us, and
- Last, but definitely not least, our heartfelt thanks go to every one of the many parents, grandparents, teachers, principals, students, and community members who allowed us to interview them for this book, either in writing or in person. You were our inspiration! May God multiply your example!

Introduction

"**I'm about to give up,** just throw in the towel!" one mother fumed her frustration over her school's rejection of an entire year's work on an abstinence-based sex education program. We felt her keen disappointment as if it were our own. To boot, she had been treated disrespectfully by members of the board of education. "Is it too late?" she asked. "Should I still keep trying or are things too far gone? I love my kids, and I don't want their faith to be destroyed." It's taken three years of research and writing to answer her.

This book will instill hope in every person who shares a deep concern for America's public schools. God hasn't given up on them and neither should we. He still has wonderful Christians faithfully working within the educational system at every level: teachers, principals, students and their parents, board members, administrators, bus drivers, lunchroom monitors, community members, and yes, even Christian bureaucrats who create school policies, do long-range planning, and administer funds. Steve has been one of them for nearly twenty-five years, but our numbers are dwindling.

Sadly, effective Christians are retreating for many reasons, ranging from fear of bodily harm on one end of the spectrum to an open disdain for the worldliness of public schools on the other. Fear and disdain seem poor companions to faith, don't you agree? Our attitude toward public schools needs to change. It's time we stepped forward by faith and helped our schools become the best they can possibly be, for the sake of our children, America's future.

Getting the Best out of Public Schools

Getting the Best out of Public Schools speaks to those who are still willing to establish themselves as agents for healthy change in the public schools. You may be a parent, teacher, youth worker, student, grandparent, or an administrator, but you know things could be a lot better. This book equips you to make a difference at every level of schooling, from relating to your child's teachers and friends to understanding the deeper issues of worldview driving current school reforms and innovations. It will help you understand how to work effectively within your local school system, know which questions to ask and of whom, and show you where you can have the greatest influence.

The insights and information within are gleaned from Steve's twenty-five years as a Christian educator, Virelle's years as an involved parent, part-time educator, and tutor, and their combined experience shepherding four of their own children through the public school system.

Yes, our schools can be a lot better, but it will take a team of committed difference makers to lift them to the absolute best that they can be: healthy school environments that provide our children with a quality education in a wholesome moral climate. With the right knowledge, effective networking, and prayer, it can happen.

Getting the Best out of Public Schools is our contribution to your best efforts. It is our prayer that God will use it to enhance your influence and magnify your example.

Chapter One

Stepping Forward Entering Your Circle of Influence

If you do not cut the moorings, God will have to break them by a storm and send you out. Launch all on God, go out on the great swelling tide of His purpose, and you will get your eyes open. If you believe in Jesus, you are not to spend all your time in the smooth waters just inside the harbour bar, full of delight, but always moored; you have to get out through the harbour bar into the great deeps of God and begin to know for yourself, begin to have spiritual discernment. **Oswald Chambers**

If any of you lacks wisdom, he should ask God, who gives generously to all without finding fault, and it will be given to him. **James 1:5**

"I don't know, Virelle, this house just doesn't feel like home. The neighborhood looks unfriendly," Steve muttered as we pulled away.

"I know the kids would miss the woods, their tree house, and all their friends. And I think the bedrooms are too small, don't you?" We moaned objections all the way home from our third major search for a different house. Everyone we found that was closer to our church and its excellent Christian school came up short. It was either too expensive or not as homey as the cozy green split-level we had moved into the year before.

Looking back, we all thought it was a miracle how God had led us there. Steve had been offered a job at the New York State Education Department at noon, and by four o'clock he called home saying he'd found the perfect house! Admittedly, that was a tough pill for Virelle to swallow at first, but the children adjusted quickly, moving from a treeless lot to a new house surrounded by beautiful woods.

The problems began when we settled into a new church and learned about its Christian school. Naturally, we thought we should try to send our children there. Our house, however, was just beyond the allowable distance for our three children to be bused to the school. We had deliberately settled in a local school district that was highly rated; still, we felt the nagging concern that our children might do better in a Christian environment. Paying tuition would require two incomes and a huge change in lifestyle, but we both worried about denying them such a privilege. So began the disappointing search for another house.

"Do you think we should keep on looking?" Virelle sighed. "Maybe God is trying to tell us something and we're missing the point."

"I think God is telling us that he wants salt in the public school, too," Steve spoke with resolve. "If you're willing to stay where we are and help our kids make a difference, I am. I believe it's where he wants us."

"I'm very willing, and I believe our kids will be, too."

Twenty-five years ago this conversation brought peace to months of agonizing in prayer over our children's education. At the time, we had just three: one in first grade, two just out of diapers. Our fourth was waiting in the wings. It was a decision that changed our lives, our family's sense of calling, and our children's lives. It also birthed "the salting principle" firmly in our minds.

The Salting Principle

Christians are feeling trampled today. In Matthew 5:13 Jesus intended us to take him seriously when he said, "You are the salt of the earth. But if the salt loses its saltiness, how can it be made salty again? It is no longer good for anything, except to be thrown out and trampled by men."

God calls his children to be a blessing to a very needy world, to reflect his character, his righteousness, and his love to others. Just as salt promotes healing and retards decay, God "salts" neighborhoods, schools, and work places with those who are willing to take a giant step forward and represent him.

Today we are thankful God gave us the courage and grace to make that choice. As a family, he carried us through countless times of testing and joy. There were plenty of both. Our four children graduated, as did their parents, with their faith stretched and strengthened. We were able to help them learn to swim upstream in today's world, to cope with resistance while maintaining their integrity, to love and pray for their non-Christian friends, and to introduce several of them and their families to Jesus Christ. It was truly a journey of faith, both thrilling and heartbreaking. Yes, we suffered at times, but today all four of our children wouldn't have had it any other way, and neither would we.

No Perfect Answers

If you are agonizing over the same decision, whether to send your children to public school, this is not a book to tell you what to do. There is no perfect way for Christian parents to educate their children. The "spiritual response" is not found in home schooling, private Christian schooling, or public schooling. God will direct each family according to its individual needs and circumstances and his calling in your life.

This is, instead, a book for those who have chosen, as we did, to become involved as salty parents with salty kids, or as salty teachers, administrators, bus drivers, or board members in your local school and community. It will equip you with the tools you will need to make a difference: knowledge of critical educational issues and current reform efforts already affecting your child, help to understand the way schools make decisions and process change, and practical, proven ways to make a difference. Folded throughout are compelling reasons to stay involved, illustrated with countless stories of Christian parents and educators whose examples and expertise are impacting America and infusing health back into "the system" known as public education.

Is It Worth It?

For some, the nagging question remains: Is it worth it? Won't schools just continue along the path of moral and academic decline no matter what we do? It's a reasonable question.

To answer it, consider by comparison bringing your child to the doctor with a list of perplexing symptoms. He's suffering from general malaise, clearly not as healthy as he once was. Restless and distracted, his vitality is gone; and with it, his interest and attention span. Clearly, he appears weak and unhealthy, whereas not long ago he seemed far more normal and exuberant.

Your doctor examines the child, shaking her head repeatedly. The prognosis doesn't look good.

"I'm sorry to inform you," she concludes, "that your child has too many health problems to be worthy of my time. There's very little use trying to help at this late stage. I'm sorry." Most of us would agree that a doctor like this should be removed from practice.

An exaggerated example? Perhaps, yet that is exactly the way many are treating the plight of America's public schools—as a sick child who can be discarded. Can we who have so freely received God's goodness, spiritual health, and vitality justify such gross disinterest in the well-being of more than 80 percent of America's children who attend public schools?

Diagnosing the Problem

Beyond a doubt, America's public schools are ill. Some are mortally wounded and may never recover. AIDS, sexual promiscuity, drug and alcohol abuse, lack of discipline, violence in schools, and even smoking are all on the rise among teenagers. Student achievement has plummeted over several decades with no sharp upturn in sight.

Symptoms of a "Sick" School

1. Attendance rate below 90%
2. Overall drop in reading scores as measured by nationwide standardized tests
3. Low percentage of graduates attending college with less than a third actually graduating
4. "Safe sex" education and condom distribution
5. Gay and lesbian agenda promoted
6. Drift from foundational truths of American history
7. Unsafe school climate
8. Pupil-to-teacher ratio higher than 30 to 1
9. High drop out and suspension rate
10. Increasing costs/decreasing student achievement/yearly defeat of annual budget
11. High teacher turnover/constant union problems
12. Unruly students/no discipline policy
13. Lack of communication with parents
14. Buildings in poor repair

Efforts at school improvement come and go, but few have demonstrated measurable positive results. Christian parents fear an illness as deadly as AIDS in today's classroom: the total absence of moral values. Like losing all your white blood cells, ill health and quite possibly death can't be far behind.

We would imagine schools in such a state might welcome helpful intervention. Ironically, it is often the case that when parents go to school to get information or answers to serious questions, they are put on the defensive and treated as intruders. One parent described the feeling as if she were walking into a bank for a loan—not much fun at all. And yet, it's our state and local tax dollars that are funding the entire operation. Far more serious, our children are the principle victims of our failing educational systems. Daily they may face hostile and potentially dangerous environments, particularly in our inner cities.

But it wasn't always this way. We once had a healthy educational system that fostered and trained business and political leaders, plumbers, builders, and electricians whose word was as good as a contract; doctors, lawyers, teachers, and judges with faith and values, who put people before privilege, fearlessly discerned right from wrong, and focused on the well-being and good of others.

A strong American educational system once accomplished that. Children learned to read using stories and primers based on clearly biblical truth. Not only did the Ten Commandments and the Constitution hang in the classroom, but teachers upheld them, taught them, sought to practice them. Communities held teachers accountable for their example to their children.

Our major colleges and universities, including Harvard, Princeton, and Yale, were founded on Christian principles. New entrants were required to sign statements of faith in Christ and attend prayer meetings or chapel. The education these students received was moral, spiritual, and values based. It outlined for life what students learned and who they became.

The Call to Return

According to Dr. Thomas Lickona, author of *Educating for Character*, moral education is the bedrock of our democracy:

> Moral education, the founders of our democracy asserted, is essential for the success of a democratic society.
>
> Their reasoning went like this: Democracy is government by the people; the people themselves are responsible for ensuring a free and just society. That means a people must, at least in some minimal sense, be good. They must understand and be committed to the moral foundations of

democracy: respect for the rights of individuals, regard for law, voluntary participation in public life, and concern for the common good. Loyalty to these democratic virtues, Thomas Jefferson argued, must be instilled at an early age.

Energized by that belief, schools in the early days of the republic tackled character education head-on. Through discipline, the teacher's good example, and the curriculum, schools sought to instruct children in the virtues of patriotism, hard work, honesty, thriftiness, altruism, and courage.[1]

Rx for Renewing Schools

Can we ever return to the health and beauty of this model? Not totally, and certainly not at all without a great many Christian parents, teachers, administrators, students, and community members involved. Together, however, we can determine to revitalize and renew our public schools to become greenhouses once again to promote healthy moral, intellectual, and spiritual growth, where parental values are affirmed and not challenged, where honesty, purity, individual worth, and the sanctity of human life are upheld for students from all backgrounds. We can make schools safe sanctuaries for building people right-side up, launch pads for lifetime learning, disciplined, violence-free environments where our children, America's children, can achieve a full measure of moral, spiritual, and intellectual health.

Reclaiming our schools will take more than wishful thinking. It will take salty, committed, informed, and persistent Christians who understand the true nature of the conflict and equip themselves to win. It's a huge task. William Bennett echoes the call in his book, *The De-Valuing of America*:

> What, then, to do? The American people face a great and important political task. They need to reassert their influence on the social institutions: elementary and secondary schools, universities, churches and synagogues, the media, the legal profession, federal, state, and local governments, and the arts. Reclaiming our institutions does not mean subjecting them to a narrow or rigid ideology; it means letting these institutions be governed by what works, by what makes sense, and by insisting that they remain true to their original purposes. In short, we need institutions that more accurately reflect the sentiments and beliefs of the great body of the American people rather than those of the cultural de-

constructionists. For the citizenry, this requires greater public scrutiny, attention, and action; institutional accountability and reform; more citizen participation (on school boards, church offices, boards of trustees, and the like); political action; and the recruitment of sympathetic talent to take jobs in, and affect the course of, these institutions. In short, we need to pay attention and act.[2]

When God Calls Us Forward

Some things haven't changed much in the last few thousand years. Those who obey God grow accustomed to finding themselves in sticky situations, where the only solution will be a miracle. It's a way of life for believers. Isaiah long ago received his commission from God much the same as we do today: He listened, he heard the call, he stepped forward. It's a story that bears repeating in Isaiah's own words:

In the year that King Uzziah died, I saw the Lord seated on a throne, high and exalted, and the train of his robe filled the temple. Above him were seraphs, . . . and they were calling to one another:
"Holy, holy, holy is the LORD Almighty; the whole earth is full of his glory."
At the sound of their voices the doorposts and thresholds shook and the temple was filled with smoke.
"Woe to me!" I cried. "I am ruined! For I am a man of unclean lips, and I live among a people of unclean lips, and my eyes have seen the King, the LORD Almighty."
Then one of the seraphs flew to me with a live coal in his hand, which he had taken with tongs from the altar. With it he touched my mouth and said, "See, this has touched your lips; your guilt is taken away and your sin atoned for."
Then I heard the voice of the Lord saying, "Whom shall I send? And who will go for us?"
And I said, "Here am I. Send me!" Isaiah 6:1–8

Was Isaiah guaranteed success? Quite the contrary; he was guaranteed a struggle. Was he sent, strengthened, encouraged, inspired, equipped, and empowered by God? You bet. Any believer in Jesus Christ who steps forward to trust God and make himself available for his purposes has the same Lord as Isaiah. It's a fact. When God directs us to step forward, we never stand alone.

Getting the Best out of Public Schools is written to equip you for the task that lies ahead. It is our prayer that you will find honesty, guidance, understanding, trustworthy information, and encouragement on these pages. We urge you to read it with the prayer that God will use you in some way to step forward in your own sphere of influence for the sake of your children as well as our great nation's families and their children.

Chapter Highlights

- No perfect answers
- Is it worth it?
- Diagnosing the problem
- Symptoms of a "sick" school
- The call to return
- Rx for renewing schools
- When God calls us forward

Key Thought

We can make schools safe sanctuaries for building people right-side up; launch pads for lifetime learning; disciplined, violence-free environments where our children, America's children, can achieve a full measure of moral, spiritual, and intellectual health.

What You Can Do

1. Think about your role in your local public schools. Ask God for an open door for effective influence.
2. Gather the facts and find out if your local schools are suffering any of the symptoms of a "sick" school as mentioned in this chapter.
3. Talk with parents, teachers, members of the board of education to learn more about your local school system and how well it is functioning.

Chapter Two

It's Not Time to Retreat! Four Compelling Reasons to Stay Involved

I think Christians must be involved in public education. I see too many Christian parents intimidated by the public schools. . . . I feel God has called me to be an educator. Each year I feel that I do make a difference in students' lives. I am excited as I become better equipped myself to be in this environment. **Greg Roberts, technology teacher**

But as for you, be strong and do not give up,
for your work will be rewarded. **2 Chronicles 15:7**

Stuart entered the conference room and sat down quietly. Now that his three children had already graduated, volunteering for another school committee wasn't his idea of fun. A neighbor had asked him to serve, knowing his background in long-range planning was needed to help the school district shape its vision statement for directing large amounts of taxpayer money to keep the schools current in a high-technology world. He shifted in his chair as he looked around the conference table at over thirty teachers and administrators. The atmosphere definitely lacked congeniality and made Stuart wish he'd stayed at home.

Shortly after the meeting was called to order by a bristly administrator, Stuart posed the question, "How many parent representatives are serving on this committee?" The question ignored, he asked it again a few minutes later. Silence again. Twice brushed aside, Stuart politely confronted the committee chairperson: "Is there some reason why I am not being permitted to know how many other parents are on this committee? How can we possibly represent the community's wishes without them?"

"There are several parents present," came the terse reply from the visibly annoyed administrator.

"How many of those parents are not employees of the district?" Stuart countered politely.

"What difference does that make?" a teacher from across the conference table shot back.

"It makes a great deal of difference when you are writing a vision statement for the future of the children of this town and using their parents' tax dollars to do it."

From that point on Stuart was regarded with suspicion and annoyance throughout the rest of the meeting. When he arrived at home two hours later, he was practically foaming at the mouth.

"Why is it that schools ignore parents? They have no interest in listening to anyone! I never thought this would happen in our own school district, this kind of hard-nosed, rationalized educational smugness. I don't even want to go back!"

"But you have to!" Stuart's wife, Katie, urged. "If you don't speak up, who will?"

"I'll just end up saying something that'll get printed in the papers. Remember the things they said about the Edwards family when their daughter refused to read a questionable book for high school English? They raked them over the coals. If I keep going to those meetings, it's bound to come out that I'm a Christian, and I'll be treated like an enemy rather than a concerned parent."

"Not if we don't treat them like an enemy," Katie added thoughtfully. "Maybe we have deserved some of the bad press we've received."

"How so?" Stuart appeared surprised.

"Well, Christians have made some pretty ugly public accusations, too. Could we have taken the wrong approach entirely? Maybe if we worked from within the system, bringing the wisdom God has given us to help and to serve the schools in a more loving way, we'd be more effective. You know, preserve the goodness from the inside out, like salt does."

"OK," Stuart smiled, pulling her over for a little hug, "perhaps it's not time to retreat, but you've got to help me. It's going to take a lot of prayer and hard work."

Perhaps you have attended similar meetings and felt much like Stuart did. You will learn more about his experiences later in the book. Christian parents these days are in a strange kettle of soup when it comes to their children's schooling. Weighing their concerns, however, and praying through them have led a growing number of these parents to join with Christian teachers, administrators, and community members who have decided not to give up the battle, but rather to work hard to reclaim America's schools. Four solid reasons motivate them:

Compelling Reason # 1: The decline of American schools and American society as we know it will not stop without Christian influence.

As godly people give up, America is on shakier ground with each passing day. The Judeo-Christian community, the salt God gave the world to represent his nature, his character, his values and love, is pulling out of public schools in droves. And where is the salt headed? Back to the salt shakers where it's safe and uncontaminated, untainted, nonthreatening. Christian parents are choosing alternative schooling for their children, either through private Christian schools, home schooling, and sometimes non-Christian private schools, when academic excellence is the driving interest. There are times when it may be the only acceptable alternative, but is it really the best overall response to the outcry over the condition of our public schools?

Granted, making a commitment to our local public school is risky. Well-known and respected Christian leaders warn us about the dangers inside those schools: Drug and alcohol abuse is rampant; gay and lesbian lifestyles are now openly accepted and advocated among both students and faculty; violence increases on high school campuses, and sexual promiscuity is resulting in epidemic numbers of sexually transmitted disease cases every year. And they are absolutely right. Schools are decaying rapidly from within. It's no secret. It's the one fact virtually everyone agrees on. Things couldn't be much worse, or could they? What if we lose the battle? What will our country be like when led by a generation of leaders educated without the influence of Christian teachers and Christian friends?

Compelling Reason # 2: This is a spiritual battle we must not lose.

It's a wonderful thing to hear our Senate and House of Representatives open their sessions with prayer. Moments later these same elected delegates pledge their allegiance to America as "one nation under God." And yet, there are many who find profound discomfort at even the mention of our biblical foundations. Their worldview is no longer God-centered, but man-centered. In most communities, biblical Christianity has sheepishly bowed out the door to the outspoken bully of secular humanism.

Our public schools have not escaped the soul-crushing blow of humanism. David Noebel, author of the comprehensive work, *Understanding the Times,* says that Christianity has been "deliberately, some would say brilliantly, erased from America's educational system. The direction of America's education can be seen as a descent from Jonathan Edwards (1750) and the Christian influence, through Horace Mann (1842) and the Unitarian influence, to John Dewey (1933) and the Humanist influence."[1] Humanism dethrones God and places man in his place. The Author and Creator of life has been shown out the door, in this case, the school door.

Parents from many differing backgrounds are beginning to recognize that this battle is a spiritual one. Christians know it is "against the rulers, against the authorities, against the powers of this dark world and against the spiritual forces of evil in the heavenly realms" (Eph. 6:12). It is heated and seemingly irrational at times because we aren't dealing with people alone. We are up against a force of darkness that highly covets the minds and values of our children, whose target is the foundation of our homes, schools, judicial system, and government: our worldview.

Why Worldview Matters to Christians

A worldview is the lens through which we look at life. No part of our lives is left unaffected by our worldview. Every decision, our ethics and values, the formation of our character, and our interpersonal relationships are shaped by our worldview. It makes a huge difference in the way our schools are run and our children are taught.

"Nothing short of a great Civil War of Values rages today throughout North America," say James Dobson and Gary Bauer. "Two sides with vastly differing and incompatible worldviews are locked in a bitter conflict that permeates every level of society."[2] Differing worldviews, as suggested by Dobson and Bauer, can help us understand some of the problems we will encounter as we try to better our public schools. In the case of the Christian, this framework is biblical, personal, and alive in Christ through the power of the Holy Spirit.

Biblical Christianity is the worldview by which believers live. Those you will be dealing with in public education may never have considered their worldview or how it impacts their lives and professions. When questioned, however, many will likely be found somewhere in the swelling ranks of the humanist camp, which houses some formidable opponents to the Christian faith.

The humanist camp has three regiments: secular humanism, Marxism/Leninism, and cosmic humanism or the New Age movement.[3] These three worldviews are in direct conflict with biblical Christianity because they remove God from his place of preeminence. Those who are interested in a complete analysis of these worldviews and how they affect our lives and culture will want to read David A. Noebel's book, *Understanding the Times* (Harvest House, 1991). For our purposes here, suffice it to say that in every serious discussion with well-educated professionals trying to better our schools, this is where the battle line will eventually be drawn. Our arch enemy, Satan, is orchestrating the opposition. Don't be surprised when you become a target. Nevertheless, we must take action. Much too much is at stake.

Compelling Reason # 3: God calls us to be salt and light.

"You know, Ellen, you are a great role model," her teacher shared in a quiet moment after class, "not just to the other students, but to me as well. I really admire the way you think and handle yourself. I'm impressed."

It was a pretty surprising statement from a high school English teacher to a seventeen-year-old senior. Ellen had maintained a quiet witness for Christ in her large urban high school. She'd even taken a lot of flack for her part in organizing a Bible club and often wondered what people thought of her for being, well, just different. Still, she was well liked and, by her senior year, she knew it.

Brad was different, and all the guys on the baseball team knew it. He didn't swear or tell off-color jokes in the locker room, didn't brag about his conquests with girls, or about being voted most valuable player two years in a row. His high academic standards and hard work in student government could have earned the reputation of a first-class geek, but the fact was, everyone liked Brad. They couldn't help it. With a warm smile and quick wit, he made everyone feel important, and his friends knew he cared.

If your kids are Christians, no doubt someone at school has taken notice, too. It's an awesome calling. When Jesus said, "All authority in heaven and on earth has been given to me. Therefore go and make disciples of all nations" (Matt. 28:18–19), he commissioned us to be his ambassadors, drawing others to him, and that includes our children. Let's be honest. Often our children put us to shame in their witness for

Christ. Is there a better place to fulfill this Great Commission than in America's public schools? Can we justify ignoring such a large mission field on our doorstep?

Over the years, many of our children's friends have found Christ simply through contacts at school, in sports, carpooling, and being invited to youth group. Some are in full-time ministry today. Others are simply learning to live lives that honor God.

When our oldest daughter began inviting one of her middle-school friends to church and youth group, it made life pretty interesting. One friend soon grew to three, and our family station wagon was bulging at the seams and noisy with the loud laughter of seven kids squeezed into a small space. Our "shuttle service" continued for years, eventually collecting kids whose home life varied dramatically from our own, but whose hearts were hungry for meaning in life and very open to God. How precious they are to us now. One boy was nearly killed a few years later in a terrible car crash that left him somewhat brain damaged; another girl went on to become full-time in the Lord's service, leading many others to Christ. We would never trade those opportunities.

The baby boomer generation continues to shape the nation's future. Today they are ushering their first wave of grandchildren to kindergarten. Will there be any Christian teachers and administrators to welcome them, or Christian classmates to play and learn with? These children and young adults will soon impact our society and nation. How about seriously involving Christ in that impact!

In his very helpful book, *Choosing Your Child's School,* David Smith strongly supports our involvement in public schools:

> Our secular society needs a legitimate Christian witness that is not afraid to tackle the many difficult problems facing all Americans. There is a place for Christians of all ages in every realm of our society, including the public schools. To collectively admit defeat and impotence by default is, I believe, a denial of the power of God to have an influence on this world through us, his servants. Jesus said that each of us is "the salt of the earth" (Matt. 5:13).[4]

Your family matters! Like salt, Christian families have a positive perspective to bring to their neighborhoods, schools, and communities; better ways of dealing with life's ups and downs, of handling conflict, of loving and caring for others. A needy world is watching. Kids who never attend church are rubbing shoulders every day with your children at school. One day it may change their lives.

Compelling Reason # 4: You are on the winning team!

In the course of writing this book we have interviewed many outstanding Christian parents, teachers, principals, students, grandparents, and community members who are actively involved in the preservation and improvement of their local public schools. They share a vision for America, similar in spirit to our founding fathers. They want a wholesome, safe, nutritive environment once again in which to raise their children and a school system that rests squarely on the strong foundation of biblical principles and family values. Like others whose hearts burn with a vision, these folk face regular opposition from liberal nay-sayers and critics. But difference makers don't quit easily.

Knowledgeable Christians such as these will have a positive impact on today's public schools and tomorrow's leaders. However, no one will hear a loving, well-thought-out biblical perspective if we leave those discussions to others. And our schools, our communities, and our nation will be the worse for it.

Christians who believe in the salting principle and are willing to remain involved in public schools can change America. Reforms in public education will come best through local individual involvement, which means you and I actively seeking improvement where we live. It isn't big government, the organized church, or a few families; it's you and me. We are the key to improving our public schools. That's what makes it such a challenging and worthy goal at the same time.

Schools resonate a nation's heartbeat and interpret its priorities to the next generation. When God is systematically eliminated from our educational system, we can be confident that our country's priorities, as we now know them, will not exist in fifty years, or even less. It's time to change that, but where do we begin?

James Dobson has dedicated his life to the preservation and strengthening of the family. His concerns have spread in recent years to many other areas of society, including our schools. He says: "The only logical solution to the problems we face as a culture is to return to the Judeo-Christian values system with which we started! This worldview bears the stamp of the Creator Himself. Our best hope is to reinstate His precepts into government, the schools and into our homes."[5]

There is not one simple way to do that. All those who share a biblical worldview are needed as salt in their particular spheres of influence. We must join hands and strengthen our influence by growing in our understanding and networking with one another to gradually bring about positive changes in our culture. It is the best formula for successful influence.

Knowledge + Networking = Positive Change

Knowledge

Become an information sponge. Read, ask questions, subscribe to quality newsletters such as those mentioned in the Resources section of this book, gain an understanding of the basic policies, reforms, innovations, and issues affecting your local school.

Networking

Share this information with others who care. Don't be afraid to initiate healthy, courteous dialogue. That's how we all grow and learn. When accurate information is shared in such a way, people often are willing to consider your point of view. You may even win some support.

Positive Change

Expect the best, but expect it to take time. Don't give up easily. Remember, knowledge shared through a growing information network is already a form of positive change. Prayer and persistence are the fuel to all successful community efforts within public schools.

"School districts," says William Bennett in his book, *The De-Valuing of America*, "don't fail or succeed nationally; they fail or succeed locally."[6] Simple advice, but profound. It's easy to get caught up in supporting national campaigns and ministries and still feel powerless to do anything about the elementary school our children attend. Local school improvement is the most significant kind there is because it affects your children and your community. We must start the process at home.

If we seriously want our local schools to respond to our initiatives for change, we must become at least reasonably conversant on major issues, involved as participants or at least as voters within the school district, and networked with other parents, grandparents, business leaders, teachers, administrators, and school board members with similar views. A book such as this can provide you with enough knowledge and practical know-how to make a difference.

A Word of Caution

One last word is needed, however, about a very critical factor, *attitude.* During the years that Steve, along with a great team of professionals, was responsible for 106 school districts, K-12, in western New York, he had many dealings with representatives of the "Christian right." He fielded many of their concerns and handled difficulties within their districts, particularly the mounting opposition to "Goals 2000," the federal grant program he helped administer. It was difficult not to publicly tell them he was a born-again Christian, too, but doing that would have violated professional ethics and weakened his effectiveness within the Education Department. Most of the people he dealt with were courteous, well-informed, sacrificial with their time, and hard working in their efforts, but a few were not. Sadly, they caused great harm to their public witness and, hence, their effectiveness statewide. It is to this handful of outspoken people that we address the following thoughts.

God has placed us in the world so that we might draw others to him, not push them away. Christ lived in the world but was not "of it." As we begin to work on the many serious problems in public education, we need to keep in mind that our words and actions represent our heavenly Father. Let's be salty enough to bring back health to the public schools but not so much that we gag people in the process. Rude and threatening language, unreasonable demands, even the quoting of Scripture inappropriately, can be destructive and undermine the prayerful efforts of countless others. The key is using words that are "full of grace, seasoned with salt, so that you may know how to answer everyone" (Col. 4:6). Then our words and our efforts will be effective and persuasive. This is easier said than done, but it is absolutely necessary.

Salty Christians, as Francis Schaeffer put it in *How Should We Then Live?* "are not only to know the right worldview, the worldview that tells us the truth of what is, but consciously to act upon that worldview so as to influence society in all its parts and facets across the whole spectrum of life, as much as we can to the extent of our individual and collective ability."[7] If you agree with Francis Schaeffer, as we do, let's equip ourselves with the knowledge and skills necessary to begin the task.

Chapter Highlights

- Compelling Reason # 1: The decline of American schools and American society as we know it will not stop without Christian influence.
- Compelling Reason # 2: This is a spiritual battle we must not lose.
- Compelling Reason # 3: God calls us to be salt and light.
- Compelling Reason # 4: You are on the winning team!

- Knowledge + Networking = Positive Change
- A word of caution: attitude

Key Thought

Christians who believe in the salting principle and who are willing to remain involved in public schools can change America. Reforms in public education will come best through local individual involvement, which means you and I actively seeking improvement where we live. It isn't big government, the organized church, or a few families; it's you and me. We are the key to improving our public schools.

What You Can Do

1. Define your own worldview. How does it impact your life goals? Parenting goals?
2 Discuss your children's ability to do well academically in school and to be a witness for Christ.
3. As you consider greater involvement in your local schools, begin a list of the names and phone numbers of others who share your concerns.
4. Subscribe to at least two or three newsletters listed in the Resources section of this book.

Chapter Three

How Salty People Behave Ten Principles for Difference Makers

My involvement in helping our school "parent" children is to be there as a parent, doing that slow but sure, bit by bit along the way. Maybe I make no difference at all, but every once in a while I hear a great story or am asked a question that verifies that it is helping. Especially when the bell rings and the halls are filled with loud, busy middle schoolers yelling out, "Hello, Mrs. K." I can't tell you the joy I feel.
Christyne Kucera, parent volunteer

Let your conversation be always full of grace, seasoned with salt, so that you may know how to answer everyone. **Colossians 4:6**

It was parents' night and Barbara had just finished giving an overview of the third-grade curriculum, touching briefly on each of the coming year's special projects to a roomful of interested parents, many of whom had requested her as their child's teacher months in advance of the school year. Her science and social studies units regularly received districtwide attention for their excellence. As a Christian teacher in a large suburban district, Barbara viewed teaching as her most significant ministry and was well respected by her colleagues. She never expected to be regarded with suspicion.

After most of the parents had asked questions, milled around the room and left, one mother hung behind the rest. "Did you have a question?" Barbara asked.

"Well, not really," the mother replied. "It's just that I wanted you to know we are strong Christians in our home, and there may be activities you have planned this year that we will exempt our daughter from if they do not meet with our approval. I expect you to understand and cooperate."

Barbara later expressed her shock coupled with a rising sense of anger at the mother's condescending attitude. "She spoke like I couldn't possibly understand, as if I were stupid and on the outside of a great enlightenment. I was truly insulted. Later, I thought, *Do I treat others like that—assuming that everyone else is a pagan before I even know them?*" It caused Barbara to reconsider the impact she as a Christian had on her peers.

Unfortunately, most of us as Christian educators, parents, and community members are guilty of the same assumptions about people and the same attitudes. How easily we slip into a "them and us" mindset when dealing with public school teachers and administrators, or parents and colleagues, even our neighbors.

As regional education coordinator for 106 school districts in western New York, Steve often found himself in the same position as Barbara. Because the most vocal group of the "Christian Right" in the state emerged from his region, he was the person most often responsible for responding to their concerns. For the most part, they were right on target—well organized, well informed, and extremely articulate, addressing issues in a courteous and timely manner. But attached to them like burrs were also loud, outspoken, and frequently rude people who regularly sought to bring down the whole educational system. Nothing pleased them more than exaggerated accusations, name-calling, and Scripture-sprinkled verbal abuse. Their unbecoming behavior drowned out the voices of the larger body of Christian parents and community members. You can imagine the negative and bristly response in the State Education Department that became associated thereafter with the phrase "Christian Right," severely hampering Steve's own credibility and efforts within the department.

Contrary to popular conservative thought, there are some outstanding good folk working within schools and education departments who are still open to parent concerns and are reasonable and willing to listen. They are driven by the sincere desire for better education within their own spheres of influence. But neither they nor anyone, Christian or not, respond well to hostile verbal abuse and a condescending attitude. In our desire for school reform, must we treat everyone with suspicion? Can we not learn to partner with schools and move hand-in-hand toward positive change without clenched fists? Learning more Christ-honoring ways of approaching our differences and concerns within our local school districts will create a healthier climate for change rather than one charged with growing tension.

Therefore, in the interest of improved relations, we suggest these ten simple standards of behavior, "salting principles" for interacting with the secular school environment, that will foster healthier discussions and more cooperative relationships. At the least, these salting principles will help us honor publicly the God we represent and demonstrate the power of infusing strong, prayerful, and godly influence in our communities.

10 "Salting" Principles for Difference Makers

1. Treat everyone with respect and courtesy.

2. Find an avenue of service and be faithful.

3. Be proactive rather than reactive.

4. Aim to be part of the solution rather than demanding one.

5. Gather accurate information rather than forming opinions based on hearsay.

6. Seek common ground, being willing to compromise on some issues.

7. Applaud your school's best efforts.

8. Never slander. Behave honorably.

9. Get involved for the long haul. Change seldom happens overnight.

10. Remember: Prayer is the *real* power behind improvement.

Let's take a closer look at each one.

1. Show courtesy and respect to everyone.

This is so basic to any interaction Christians have in the world, it hardly seems worth mentioning. Yet parents who feel the school is undermining their family's religious convictions or values have been known to shout down their opponents at school board meetings, storm unannounced into classrooms, and write angry and sarcastic letters to teachers, administrators, and newspapers. All of us at one time or another have felt our necks get hot with anger over some unjust action a teacher took with our children. Even when classroom situations warrant swift, decisive action, we need to handle them with courtesy, salted with strong conviction and respect that reveals great strength.

James 1:19–20 speaks directly to Christians in conflict: "My dear brothers, take note of this: Everyone should be quick to listen, slow to speak and slow to become angry, for man's anger does not bring about the righteous life that God desires." Rather, our anger implies God isn't strong enough to "fix things" for us and we have to do it ourselves. Enough said? Stay cool in your next confrontation, pray like mad, communicate clearly, and trust God to act.

Sally and Ed Dix certainly had their faith tested in this regard. It was November in a fourth-grade year that already felt far too long for their daughter, Erin. Her teacher was a woman with a tight agenda and a short fuse. Erin's struggle was math, and with the introduction of "new math" in their district a few years previous, she was having tremendous difficulty keeping up. To further complicate matters, Erin was a shy nine-year-old who hated to draw attention to herself. Following a math lesson one day, while all the class was breezing through a work sheet, Erin ventured to the teacher's desk at the front of the room to ask for help. It was a big mistake.

After repeatedly explaining the math problem in an increasingly loud voice without the results she wanted, the teacher grabbed Erin's hair by the bangs and pulled her head right down to the paper. Tears stung the little girl's eyes while the whole roomful of fourth graders stared in amazement, some even snickering. It was one of the worst moments of her young life.

Needless to say, when Sally and Ed heard this story that evening, they wanted to march into school the next day and pull that teacher's hair right out of her head. Instead, they decided to pray about it first as a family, soothe their daughter's bruised spirit, and sleep on it. The next morning during their devotions, these verses from James regarding anger spoke directly to their dilemma. They made an immediate appointment to meet with the teacher and the principal, received an apology, as did Erin, and a promise that it would never happen again. Needless to say, something similar did happen within a few weeks, and the principal quickly moved to have Erin transferred that day to another classroom with Mr. Lawrence, who soon became one of her favorite teachers. Had the Dixes been rude or disrespectful the first time, it is doubtful they would have received such instant compliance with their request. God will always make a way through the problem when we follow his lead.

2. Be faithful in your service.

Even the words are like music to a tired teacher. Whether you volunteer in the library once a week, type students' compositions for a school literary magazine, or carpool for class trips, any effort to help your child's school delivers a big message, "I care and I deliver what I promise."

What can two working parents or one exhausted single parent possibly do to help? Many things. Vote for candidates you believe in, stay well informed, write notes of appreciation, supervise homework, attend all of your child's concerts, plays, and sporting events, make time for parent-teacher conferences, and network with other parents.

Involvement is an essential prerequisite for responsiveness. When she served as education policy manager at Focus on the Family, Linda S. Page brought many years of experience as a teacher and administrator to her job. She strongly advocates that parents find some avenue of involvement even if it's not completely welcome at first:

> Involvement in key school issues may be difficult to achieve, since some teachers and administrators view parental involvement in curriculum and instruction as "meddling" or as "being a nuisance." Some teachers and administrators assume that once the child comes to school, the responsibility for education belongs exclusively to them, and that parental involvement should be limited to support for their programs. Perhaps some educators have forgotten that parents are ultimately responsible for their children's education. . . . Parents are the only ones who are most highly motivated to see their children succeed.[1]

Some parents demonstrate a level of faithfulness most of us would find staggering. Marci had always been involved in the education of her three children as a class parent, had assisted in school activities, and had attended board meetings and school functions. When she noticed the unusual turnover of teachers and superintendents, she decided to investigate further. About the same time, her fourth-grade son, Kevin, began having problems in school. She visited his teacher, who appeared to be floundering badly in her first year on the job. Marci rolled up her sleeves and got involved. It was like turning over a rock and finding a host of problems that had been kept out of sight. We'll let her tell you the rest of the story:

> After a number of conferences with Kevin's teacher, I was repeatedly told that when he improved in reading comprehension his grades would improve. I asked over and over again what I could be doing to assist him, and always the same response. In fifth grade he had another new, first-year teacher. I became a room-parent, talked frequently with the teacher, and tried to get a feel for how the class was being conducted. The class was very loosely structured and I wondered what, if anything, was being learned. Again, I inquired about Kevin's lack of progress and was told he could be tested to see if he had a learning disability. The testing stalled to a point and never did happen. After that year, I was very discouraged and not at all opti-

mistic about what the next year would bring. It seemed to me that in spite of my efforts, Kevin's education was going nowhere, and nobody seemed to care in the public system.

The following August, there was a very intense board meeting. The main issue centered around the frequent hiring and firing of teachers, leaving the school in a constant state of change. Out of forty teachers, half were "let go" over a three-year period. At that time, I strongly voiced my concerns to the board about the severe *lack of education* affecting my son. For example, only half of the math text was covered, and about ten chapters of the social studies book that year. I said that I felt that Kevin had missed the equivalent of a whole year of education over a two-year period and was falling through the cracks of the system. I expressed concern that changes be made so that this didn't happen again and affect other students beyond the class that he was in. I keenly felt the disapproval of the board members and administrators for stating these facts publicly. They felt I just didn't know what I was talking about.

The following September, things began to look better, but only briefly. A new teacher arrived on the scene. I wondered how this teacher was going to take this "motley" group of undisciplined, unlearned sixth graders and try to "catch them up" because of all they had missed. Mrs. Frank was energetic, progressive, and positive in her overview of the year. She was the best thing that had ever happened to this class. She took a hands-on approach to education, pushing the kids to reach and learn and get excited about expanding their minds. After four months the administration actively pursued getting rid of her over a technicality involving a routine extension for her certification. I sincerely believe that she was thought of as a liability to the school because she was not easily "controlled" and was very independent in her methods of teaching. She was removed and replaced midyear with the sister of a board member.

After the transition, I asked to observe the classroom to get a feel for how my son was handling the change of teachers. It took several weeks for this to be accomplished without any real cooperation from the principal and the new teacher. In effect, I was being blacklisted as a trouble maker.

Most of us would have quit by now. Not Marci. She spent months investigating other decisions the superintendent and board had made, uncovering evidence of illegal and imprudent management that went as far as the state's commissioner of education for review. In addition, she networked with other parents who shared her concerns and worked hard to have responsible, conservative candidates elected to the board. A number of years later, things have changed dramatically, including her son's education.

Kevin eventually connected with some better teachers and, with a little extra help, boosted his reading level and his confidence level. He was recently inducted into the National Honor Society, "a tangible reward for his diligence and perseverance over the past seven years," his mother said, smiling broadly.

Like every school in America, there have been an assortment of problems over the years, with textbooks that conflicted with family values, the sex education curriculum, and a gay principal who used his influence to promote a gay and lesbian agenda. Marci's willingness to conduct responsible dialogue with the school, to work faithfully on solutions, and to seek opportunities to serve her district in very positive ways are making a big difference in her small community. Some people still view her as a troublemaker, but most are gaining courage to speak up and are learning from her example.

Don't assume that as a taxpayer in your child's school district your voice will be heard when a problem or concern arises. It's not only the wheel with the loudest squeak that gets the most attention. More often, it's the well-oiled, dependable wheel that has helped keep the system running. Your voice carries long and far when you are recognized as a faithful, supportive parent in many matters, rather than just a critic in some.

3. Be proactive rather than reactive.

Letter-writing campaigns, picketing, and protests of all sorts have their place. We have actively participated in many forms of peaceful protest over the years, but the most far-reaching and constructive approach is to be proactive in school reform, focusing your attention in areas of special interest or concern to you. Serve on school committees that are choosing curricula, library books, or health education materials *before* final decisions are made. Get to know your school board members, teachers, and administrators, even the local representatives of teacher unions and professional organizations (Yes, you heard it right! They are important people to know.), and join the PTA or PTO. Develop good working relationships ahead of time, even in small ways, making certain your beliefs and concerns are expressed in a Christ-honoring way.

Being busy is everyone's excuse, but there's always something you can do. Whether a lot or a little, it all adds up. One mother we spoke to serves as eighth-grade parent representative for the Parent/Team Committee, the Shared Decision Making Team, and the Character Counts committee. In addition, substituting frequently as a cafeteria aide allows her to know all her children's friends well and pray for them.

Pretty impressive for a mom who also runs a golf pro shop part time! Even doing just one of those things faithfully would make a difference.

The bottom line is this: Becoming more proactive is about being salt in our public schools, preservers of goodness, like Marci, before they rot completely from within. It's about influence, about restoring reverence for Judeo-Christian values and a biblical worldview, before secular humanism or moral relativism is allowed to soak through all the remaining fibers of our culture. It's about adding the voice of wisdom to our planning and decision making, and applauding excellence in art and culture and literature. It's about creating a thirst for truth in those who learn to trust our judgment because they see truth in the way we live and conduct our lives. Being proactive is the only way to protect our nation's greatest resource, our children, from the valueless nether world of moral and mental decay growing like yeast throughout our nation.

4. Be part of the solution rather than demanding one.

This could be called the "Finger-in-the-Dike Principle." A proactive person is a problem solver. Rather than wait for someone else to stick a finger in the widening gap, he asks, What is the problem? and What can I do to help?

The computer lab in a small elementary school had no one to run it and no funds available to pay for technical help. Every day in the darkened classroom twenty or more donated computers collected dust. That is, until ten-year-old Roseanne went home and told her daddy, a computer whiz. Within a day Bob Ventura volunteered to set up all the computers, train both teachers and students in how to use them, and be available to help and answer questions one day a week, provided someone could help open the boxes and plug the computers in. You see, Bob is a quadriplegic. He is also a problem solver, a lifesaver to that elementary school, and a hero to his daughter.

Sadly, many school districts don't want parent involvement in school improvement. Administrators feel threatened by questions and outside input and may allow parents to serve on committees only in superficial ways. Susan described her experience on a high school semestering committee as a token role, only a "step above baking cookies," allowed more to pacify her as a parent representative than to solicit her advice.

One teacher on such a committee even said, "Parents should leave us alone and allow us to do our job." If teaching were just a job, that might be an allowable statement, but it isn't. Christian or not, a teacher's job shapes our children's lives, and parents must be allowed to question and offer their input. The most effective parents and teachers will seek solutions that are mutually acceptable.

Technology teacher Greg Roberts suggests taking the time to develop good relationships with schools. "The most effective parents are the ones who have been involved in school activities and have also shown concerns for students. Parents must be able to suggest things that may work and not just condemn." Whenever we seek constructive solutions and get in there and help accomplish them, we have earned the right to be heard in the future.

5. Gather correct information.

It was Thursday evening when Steve received a phone call that a lesbian attorney and gay rights activist had been invited to address our high school student body on Friday morning to promote tolerance and acceptance of the gay lifestyle. Parents had not been informed, and thus had not been allowed to keep their children from attending the assembly. Steve decided to check it out. Since our own children had already graduated from high school, he called the parents of all the high school students on our street. No one knew about it and all were concerned about the appropriateness of such an assembly, some even angered. Next, Steve called the superintendent of schools. Even he did not know about the speaker coming to the high school. Who had sponsored her? Who would pay her? Did the other teachers know about this? By early next morning, parents had networked and flooded the high school switchboard with over a hundred calls and brought enough pressure to bear on the principal to opt their children out of the assembly.

Steve's presence was obviously viewed with some degree of nervousness and suspicion when he took the morning off from work and appeared at the assembly, a Dictaphone in his pocket, a school board member at his side. He was shocked at what he heard, a graphic, even humorous glorification of the gay and lesbian lifestyle complete with a gay former student giving a testimony. However, his recording of the whole assembly, and careful gathering of information, provided clear evidence when he confronted the board of education at a public meeting several days later. Every television news channel was there as Steve delivered an impassioned denunciation of the event. For an entire week clips of his statements were aired over and over on daytime and evening news. The editorial pages of our newspapers were full of letters from parents, students, and teachers protesting the assembly. Thankfully, this led to a policy statement within our district promising parents a more careful review process in the future and an opportunity to exempt their children from assemblies they considered inappropriate. Someone listened and cared.

You don't need a college degree to be well informed. Sue Petrinic, a mother of three in western New York, often felt intimidated when approaching school officials because she didn't have a college education. Then about five years ago she recognized her need to learn more about what was going on. She subscribed to six or seven newsletters and information sources that reflected the efforts of large-scale information gatherers who shared her values. Today Sue understands better than most educators the subtle innuendoes of outcome-based education (OBE), health and sex education, and Goals 2000. In fact, recently a teacher friend in another district called her to ask for a clear explanation of OBE! Good information leads to good influence.

It takes faith and persistence to find the opportunities waiting behind the more obvious dangers in today's public schools. But those opportunities represent people, lives waiting to be changed and enriched. Turning away from them is difficult to justify.

6. Seek common ground.

One thing Sue learned early in her school involvement was the value of an open forum in seeking consensus on any issue. People with many different views can usually agree on some things, even if they seem small at the time. Expressing our views publicly, with accurate information, gives opportunity for listeners of different persuasions to consider where they might be in agreement and causes more support to surface. Seeking common ground means we are not simply trying to win a debate; rather, we are seeking an ongoing dialogue and a more productive relationship with those who oppose our views.

"No one needs to be hated even if we do not accept people's lifestyles," Sue said emphatically. Part of the anger generated by the gay and lesbian assembly in our own district was fueled by despicable name-calling and foul-mouthed put-downs of those who found their choices repulsive. These attitudes are totally unacceptable for Christians who want to be salt in their communities. We are called to show God's love to others, whether we approve of their lifestyles or not, but that doesn't mean being a passive pushover on standards of moral purity.

7. Applaud your school's best efforts.

Before they ask you to rewrite your term paper, the best teachers will begin by telling you two positive comments for every negative. Knowing their aim is to grow a better writer makes the criticism easier to swallow. It's not a bad maxim for any learning relationship. In dealing with children or their teachers, whether you are a parent or administrator, doors of communication open best when oiled with well-deserved praise.

In his book, *The De-Valuing of America*, William Bennett underlines this sentiment: "Many ordinary people in our schools already perform magnificently; if schools were properly organized, and good people were allowed and encouraged to rise to the top, there could be many more magnificent ones. Ordinary people are capable of extraordinary things."[2] Good teachers should be recognized and rewarded publicly and privately. Poor teachers should not be rewarded, but corrected privately. If warranted, they should be removed from their classrooms, which is the best reason on earth for abolishing tenure, or at least limiting it.

If you are seeking influence in your local school district, please don't ignore the many noble, creative, hard-won victories of kids and teachers that happen every day. Applaud the best. Deal wisely with the rest.

8. Never slander. Behave honorably.

Following closely on the heels of well-deserved applause is the caution against slander or unjustified public accusations. In Titus 3:1–2 we are admonished "to be ready to do whatever is good, to slander no one, to be peaceable and considerate, and to show true humility toward all men." Unfortunately, that isn't always the case.

"There are some Christian groups out there who make me ashamed. They are so militant and unloving." Suzy's comments reflected many of those we interviewed. How unbecoming! Yet, how easy to be that way.

In her classic book, *Out of the Saltshaker and into the World*, Rebecca Manley Pippert talks about the difficulty we all have loving an often unlovable world:

> In order to establish trust with people we must love them with the baggage they bring with them. We need to accept them where they are without compromising our Christian standards.
>
> We, too, must live with the tension of being called to identify with others without being identical to them.[3]

In order to avoid making the same mistakes, Suzy's advice was: "Form a network of parents who care and lovingly but firmly work as a unit toward change. Use phone chains and on-line services, write constructive letters to the editor of your local paper, invite guest lecturers for a public forum. Just don't give up and retreat!" The stakes are too high and we have too much to lose.

9. Get involved for the long haul. Change seldom happens overnight.

Chris is a parent who is deeply committed to making a difference in education. Recently she shared, "I feel very strongly that the Christian family's role in our public schools is our only true hope. Getting involved at all levels very early on is, I feel, life-changing for our schools." And yet, discouragement is a regular enemy to continued effort. It's not uncommon for concerned parents to pull their children out of public school after one or two years of serving on committees, making an effort to become well informed, and taking a stand on an important issue. Then comes a major setback and they quit. Many choose private schools or home schooling as their solution. As helpful as those choices may seem, they are only short-term solutions to a very big problem that won't go away. Over 80 percent of America's children still attend the schools they just gave up on. Who will be there for them on Monday morning?

There are valid arguments in some circumstances for withdrawing your children from public school while still maintaining an influence there yourself. In some cases, it may be clearly the best choice. However, rarely do parents continue their involvement in the ongoing issues related to public schools when their children are educated elsewhere. There simply isn't enough time to do it all. Becoming an effective, positive force within the local school takes time, and surprisingly, our children often have a bigger impact than their parents. They are there all day and their training, faith, and personhood speak volumes.

One of the best things parents can do is to prepare their children well for their public school experience and then stay closely involved with them on a daily basis. There is no substitute for good parenting. Even the best school system in America can never replace that, but who can measure the far-reaching effect of good parents partnered with good schools? The blessing goes far beyond our immediate families and touches the whole nation and even the world.

10. Prayer is the *real* power behind improvement.

Moms in Touch is a nationally growing movement of moms in each community who meet weekly to pray for their children's teachers, fellow students, and coaches. What could be more important than that? They are typically a small group of tenacious, loving, and concerned women who are very involved in their school and meet weekly with one agenda: to pray for their school. I question whether any force of spiritual darkness could stand long when confronted by a Moms in Touch group of prayer warriors. By "adopting" teachers, coaches, and administrators, even students, they move mountains of resistance to biblical values, smooth out tensions, support the timid, encourage those on the front lines of school reform and the shaping of young minds. Who wouldn't want them on their team? (Can "Dads in Touch" or "Grandparents Who Care" groups be far behind?)

Recently I heard of a coach who contacted a local Moms in Touch group and asked them to pray him through the season's basketball games. Currently one local group is making an effort to see that all coaches use language on the court and on the field that eliminates profanity and builds kids up rather than tears them down. Quietly, lovingly, consistently they are making a difference. Applaud them. Even better, join them.

Prayer brings every one of these ten Salting Principles into focus. Without prayer, they are only good efforts, or rather, efforts to be good. With prayer, they are empowered by God. Be advised, however, that those who have begun to pray have joined the battle to reclaim America's schools.

Chapter Highlights

10 principles for difference makers:

- Treat everyone with respect and courtesy.
- Find an avenue of service and be faithful.
- Be proactive rather than reactive.
- Aim to be part of the solution rather than demanding one.
- Gather accurate information rather than forming opinions based on hearsay.
- Seek common ground, being willing to compromise on some issues.
- Applaud your school's best efforts.
- Never slander. Behave honorably.
- Get involved for the long haul. Change seldom happens overnight.
- Remember: Prayer is the *real* power behind improvement.

Key Thought

The bottom line is this: Becoming more proactive is about being salt in our public schools, preservers of goodness, like Marci, before they rot completely from within. It's about influence, restoring reverence for Judeo-Christian values, and a biblical worldview before secular humanism or moral relativism is allowed to soak through all the remaining fibers of our culture.

What You Can Do

1. Ask yourself honestly if you might be guilty of a "them and us" mentality. Examine your own relationships with your local school. Are your children learning from your example to conduct themselves in ways that are healthy, honoring to God, proactive, and prayerful? If a note of apology is called for, just do it, and move forward with a better stride.
2. Have you visited your child's school, attended a school board meeting, spoken at open forums, voted in the last school board election? Ask yourself, what's the next step for me? Expressing appreciation?
3. Become a gatherer of accurate information. Check out the Resources section at the end of this book and sign up for several newsletters. Even if you are a teacher in your district and are a little uncertain what your district's policies and philosophies are regarding areas of concern to you, ask questions. Find the decision makers and voice your concerns. Ask how you can become involved on policy-making committees.
4. Get to know your school board members, children's teachers, and administrators, and yes, even your union representative. Network with parents who care about family values, curriculum, and student achievement. Express your concerns along with your willingness to be involved in seeking solutions.

Chapter Four

Values Every School Can Uphold Building Character in the Classroom

If the family has been usurped by today's schools, it is because the family has allowed it. The busy parent or the absent parent has conveniently allowed the school to take on his/her responsibilities. Someone must raise that child. If the family is negligent and the church is not a strong influence, then the school will naturally take over.
Debbie McCoy, fifth-grade teacher

In everything set them an example by doing what is good. In your teaching show integrity, seriousness and soundness of speech that cannot be condemned, so that those who oppose you may be ashamed because they have nothing bad to say about us. **Titus 2:7–8**

Recently a teacher friend shared, "This was my worst year of teaching after more than twenty years. I had a group of about ten kids who bickered with each other like buckshot. They were used to doing it! Worse than that, most of these kids didn't take any responsibility for their actions. They felt no sense of ownership when they did things that were wrong. Some of their parents were just as frustrated with them as I was and appreciated any help I could give them."

She went on to describe a typical incident in her elementary school classroom where a week-long class art project had been partly destroyed by a child who came running full speed into the classroom and slid into the entire collection of drying paper maché puppets, leaving many of them broken.

"I couldn't help it," he said. "It's not my fault. I just fell. Call someone to clean it up."

"He expressed no remorse for the damage his actions had caused to other students' work, and assumed no responsibility to make amends," my friend fumed. "Needless to say, I made him clean it up, apologize to the other students, and help them fix their puppets. Unfortunately, this type of behavior is becoming very common in school. I've always enjoyed teaching, but now I'm not looking forward to next year."

Along with whatever else is wrong with America's schools, there is the looming backdrop of moral decline. Ask any teacher. Year after year a new crop of students files into her classroom with an increasingly vague sense of right and wrong. Riding piggyback on an already weighty curriculum is the growing burden to teach basic values once considered a universal standard in American homes. Values like honesty, integrity, courtesy, respect for authority and the rights and property of others, pride in workmanship, and a reverence for high academic standards seem frighteningly absent. Schools are left to pick up the pieces of broken family life, serious social and emotional problems, overworked or absentee parents, and weakened character training at home. Is it the responsibility of teachers to do that? Of course not. Moral education belongs squarely with parents, but the reality is, more often than not, no one is teaching values at home as loudly as the radio and TV.

Christians are certainly not alone in their concerns. Most of America is singing the same song. Listen to the tune of a recent Gallup Poll regarding public attitudes toward our schools:

> "The fundamental tragedy of American education is not that we are turning out ignoramuses, but that we are turning out savages," says Frederick Close, director of education for the Ethics Resource Center in Washington, D.C. . . . He echoes the sentiments found in a growing body of literature that includes the best-selling *Book of Virtues* by William Bennett, who used his office of secretary of education in the late eighties to campaign for "moral literacy" in the public schools. . . . Like many of his fundamentalist backers, Bennett believes that we must recover paradigms that we once shared as a nation "before the triviality of television absorbed most of children's attention and before a prevailing cynicism made virtue seem laughable."[1]

Debbie McCoy is a devoted Christian who clearly sees teaching as her calling, but it's not easy. For the past fifteen years she has welcomed tomorrow's leaders into her suburban fifth-grade classroom. The faces look much the same, but the kids inside are different. When asked whether the disruption of the American family necessitated a stronger role in the teaching of character and values by the public school, Debbie responded: "Unfortunately, yes. During the past ten years I have become increasingly aware of the fact that children are not being trained in character development at home. Their values reflect what they view (TV, magazines, electronic games) and what they hear (TV, radio, music). Their role models should come from within their own families. I tell my parents, 'Some strong influence is going to develop your child's conscience. Will it be the media, their peer group, or you?'" You will hear more from Debbie in chapter 11.

Dr. Tom Lickona, author of *Educating for Character,* has been affectionately referred to by some in his field as the "Betty Crocker of values education." He sees the role of the school as a partner in the moral development of children along with parents and religious training:

> A society needs values education both to survive and to thrive—to keep itself intact, and to keep itself growing toward conditions that support the full human development of all its members. Historically, three social institutions have shared the work of moral education: the home, the church, and the school. In taking up values education, schools are returning to their time-honored role, abandoned briefly in the middle part of this century.[2]

Teaching values in schools today is risky business, however, and guaranteed to raise the ire of more than one community group, not just Christians. The fact that it is such a universal concern means we don't have to look much further than values to find not only common ground but fertile soil for dialogue. But tread carefully. It is a landscape dotted with land mines. It helps to be well prepared and pay attention to words of caution from Christian teachers who are daily living out their faith in the school environment.

Greg Roberts, a high school technology teacher, has this to say: "I see society wanting the schools to take over the role of the family. I don't think that's something the schools want to do. . . . If parents are not careful, the school will have much more of an influence on their children than they want. They must cultivate a strong relationship with their children at home. It is not really schools that have the most influence on students. It is their peers. Have parents done a good job in equipping their children to deal with these people?" Greg sees character education as a perfect open door for "equipped Christian parents to get involved and make a difference."

This chapter will lead you through the landscape of values and character education, let you know some good work that is already being done as well as point out "red flag" areas, and give you handles on how to make a difference in your community. First, let's start with a few basics.

Semantics, the study of meaning in language, plays a huge role in a discussion as confusing and emotionally laden as the one surrounding values. A few definitions are necessary. A look at *Webster's Seventh New Collegiate Dictionary* yields some interesting information.

- A *value* is defined as something having "relative worth, utility or importance; degree of excellence." It is surprising to note that it carries not a shred of religious overtone.

- A *virtue* is described as "conformity to a standard of right; a particular moral excellence." Virtues, to the Christian mind, imply traits that please God. In today's marketplace, they are simply standards of generic goodness.

- *Morals* refer more specifically to an outside standard and are defined as "relating to principles of right and wrong in behavior, sanctioned by or operative on one's conscience or ethical judgment." One's moral judgment must be derived from a concept of truth. While the humanist argues truth is relative, the biblical Christian knows that truth emanates from the character of the living God as revealed in Scripture. Teaching moral principles apart from biblical truth presents, for Christians, an immediate conflict.

- *Character* is defined as "one of the attributes or features that make up and distinguish the individual; reputation, moral excellence and firmness."[3] Character, then, is the application of values, virtues, and morals in individual life; in other words, the finished product.

Why This Matters to Christians

It is the shaping of a child's character that is of greatest concern to most parents, particularly Christians. There is a distinct line between upholding standards of good and right behavior and teaching moral judgments that do not emerge from the character of God and his commandments.

Therefore, approaching the whole idea of teaching values, morals, and good character in schools is a critical discussion that Christians have an obligation to enter. Next, we must take a good look at what's been happening so far.

Values Clarification: A Giant Step Backward

Part of the current tidal wave of reform called outcome-based education, or OBE, is the nebulous area called values clarification. Rooted in the early seventies, values clarification encouraged children to clarify their own values. There are no absolutes.

For example, a typical scenario might be a discussion of a personal sense of pride. "What makes you feel proud?" the teacher asks. Answers vary from "playing the violin," to "making a goal in soccer," to "my daddy is a doctor." Pretty predictable answers until the next kid chortles, "I'm proud that I can whip anybody's butt!" In an effort to be value-neutral, teachers find themselves in the awkward position of being a nonjudgmental listener, trained to avoid a moral judgment even in a clear-cut situation.

"Is that a good idea?" the teacher sidesteps. "What do you think, class?" Again, William Bennett said it best, "This form of relativism said, in effect, that no set of values was right or wrong; everybody had an equal right to his own values; and all values were subjective, relative, personal."[4] In other words, if it seems OK to you, do it, whether it's cheating on a test because you didn't have time to study, or being rude to a teacher you think is a jerk anyway, or aborting a baby so nobody has to know you've been having sex since you were twelve. The thinking is, if it doesn't bother me, why should it bother you?

In his book, *Our Hopes Our Dreams,* Gary Bauer, president of the Family Research Council in Washington, D.C., expresses his outrage:

> Haven't we had enough of fads? Just recall the foolishness that has penetrated our classrooms in the last 20 years. Values clarification stripped actions bare of ethical content and encouraged students to supply their own meaning. The self-esteem movement told the young to value themselves, not as children of God with the duty to discover their hidden talents, but as some kind of unique expression of the genetic code, with no particular responsibility to anyone but themselves.[5]

Should we be surprised, then, at today's value-neutral generation that produces kids capable of committing horrendous crimes without guilt, crimes like brothers conspiring to murder both parents, and gangs who rape, slash, and leave a young woman for dead as Saturday night fun?

If teachers are to be nonjudgmental listeners, upholding values in schools will be nearly impossible. Communities, schools, teachers, and parents must come to an agreement that this foolishness has to end. There are right and wrong judgments that are mutually agreeable and good for society. It's time school administrators stopped being such cowards, terrified of lawsuits from parents, and uphold what's right and good.

Is Character Education the Answer?

Certainly something must be done. Most of us agree that the celebration of honesty, integrity, hard work, good citizenship, compassion, and fairness is sorely needed in today's schools, not simply to be taught, but demonstrated in the lives of faculty and administrators. Why is teaching character in school a problem? Simply because character is the application of values and faith on our ethical standards, our integrity. Both school and community must agree on which character traits to emphasize and how to define them. That's no longer an easy task given the diversity in this country.

HELP WANTED IMMEDIATELY:

TEACHERS WITH INTEGRITY

This country has a critical need for teachers with strong character and high integrity. Students need models of wholesome thinking. They need to know that biblical perspective makes good sense and is defensible.

High school technology teacher Greg Roberts shares how he finds continual opportunities to open the minds of his students on controversial issues. "As a teacher, I try to let students realize that there are people who do have opposing views on abortion, sexuality, free speech, marriage. Most students never hear these alternatives because the Christians do not oppose them openly or with credibility. There are not many Christian students who have been equipped to take a stance."

The teaching of character cannot be separated from the one doing the teaching, and that makes a lot of people uncomfortable. Many teachers, unsure of their own worldview and values, are finding it full of self-exposure and extremely difficult. Where character is concerned, it is very difficult to teach what you don't live. For example, when a rookie science teacher corrected her junior high student for swearing in class by saying, "That's inappropriate language, and it's not allowed," the young man returned, "Why not? The substitute teacher swore at us today."

Even the best curriculum for character education will appear weak, even silly, when taught by someone of questionable character himself. Nearly every community has suffered from some experience with a teacher misusing the trust of the children in his or her charge. How much longer can the teaching profession allow their ranks to be dishonored by a wholesale disregard for sexual misconduct, drug and alcohol abuse, and public use of profane language among their peers? It's time teachers, board members, and principals expected higher standards of conduct in their own profession. Yet, in spite of the fact that we are all very imperfect people, something must be taught. The question is, what?

One Community's Solution: The Constitution

Teaching character in the classroom with strength and conviction is a natural open door for Christians to be salt in their local school. It is also the place for the meeting of minds and spirits within the community where parents, clergy, students, senior citizens, educators, and businessmen can best find common ground.

A search for common ground led the citizens of Baltimore, Maryland, back to the Constitution and the Bill of Rights. What better meeting place for both the Christian and mainstream community? With representatives of nearly every major ethnic and religious group on the committee, diversity became their greatest reason for success. Searching through the foundational tenets of our country, they found twenty-four values that were either explicit or implicit in the Constitution:

Compassion	Courtesy
Critical Inquiry	Due Process
Equality of Opportunity	Freedom of Thought & Action
Honesty	Human Worth & Dignity
Integrity	Justice
Knowledge	Loyalty
Objectivity	Order
Patriotism	Rational Consent
Reasoned Argument	Respect for Others' Rights
Responsibility	Responsible Citizenship
Rule of Law	Self-Respect
Tolerance	Truth[6]

Parents, educators, and community members may use a list such as this to derive a list of ten or twelve essential, or core, values their district can celebrate and uphold. One school chose to emphasize three core values a year on a four-year rotating basis, including everyone from office staff to coaches. They included staff development and a resolve to implement these values in every character-related decision from the board of education to the kindergarten teacher. After all, "young America" is watching and they can spot a hypocrite lightning-fast.

Programs You Can Trust

There are already fully developed curricula for teaching character that have been endorsed by prominent educators, political figures, and religious leaders. Among them is *Character Counts,* a product of the Josephson Institute in Marina del Rey, California, which structures a program around six values, or pillars of character: trustworthiness, respect, responsibility, fairness, caring, and citizenship.

When Chris Kucera, a parent volunteer, helped seventh-grade students in her local school paint a mural honoring a fellow student who died of leukemia, the idea grew to another mural illustrating the six pillars of their Character Counts program and included inspirational quotes from great American leaders. Research has shown that children will reach for a higher standard when it is clearly presented and modeled by adults. Many schools have reported significant increases in student performance corresponding with an emphasis on character and values.

Another program that has received international attention is *Children of the World* and its public and private school component, the *North American School Project.* It is a character education curriculum that is unique in its emphasis on worldview. It is a curriculum already requested in Russian schools, in Venezuela, and in Malani, Africa, and is currently being adapted for use in secular schools in this country. Information and sample lessons can be obtained by contacting the address found in the Resources section at the end of this book.

Another well-recommended award-winning character education program is *Values in Action,* developed by Gene Bedley, a national PTA Educator of the Year. A comprehensive seven-year program, it integrates seven values into the entire school climate: respect, compassion, integrity, positive mental attitude, cooperation, initiative, and perseverance. Listings of all these programs, as well as others, can be found in the Resources section of this book. Christian parents and educators should leap for joy at the tremendous resources available to them. There are excellent people pouring their lives into the healthy, wholesome, and biblical development of character and values of today's children and tomorrow's leaders.

Green Light for Action

If a sense of caution still remains regarding character education, *consider two things:*

1. *Who should make the decision* and choose the materials used?
2. *How can you best use your influence* to see that excellent character education materials are used in your own school district?

It is critically important that Christians become involved in guiding the development of all character education programs. Parents may find Chris Kucera's suggestion helpful to offer "positive reinforcement to godly issues without using the word *godly.*" The soundest approach is often to limit the values a school teaches to those affecting your child's education, such as honesty, integrity, respect for authority, the value of hard work, academic excellence, responsibility, courtesy, fairness, etc. It is the responsibility of parents, along with their churches, to teach the biblical basis for a highly moral character, a God-centered worldview. No one should trust their public school to do that. However, we can and must expect our local schools to uphold those values that are of greatest relevance in the academic environment while honoring a parent's right to teach moral and religious values at home.

A Word About Tolerance

Those who speak from a Judeo-Christian worldview are often accused of being intolerant of those who don't share their view, particularly by the gay and lesbian community. We are often described as narrow-minded, having about as much enlightenment as those in the Flat Earth Society. How are we to handle the gold-plated "tolerance" agenda that elevates moral relativism rather than the absolutes of the Ten Commandments? We can emphasize the fact that tolerance does not mean an absence of standards, but rather patience with others who deviate from that standard and commitment to work together to maintain agreed-on standards. Does that mean relaxing our moral values, accepting a flagrant disregard for right and wrong? Hardly, but using our values as a club does little to win others to our position. Pray for courage and discernment to be a spokesperson in your sphere of influence should God give you an opportunity.

The bottom line is, if we are not salt, what will be the lasting effect on the next generation of community, state, and national leaders now in public school? The greater risk is in refusing to stand for what is right. All over the country, as parents and educators, business and professional leaders are struggling with the same concerns, many are stepping up to the plate to say, "I care what's happening to our values in today's schools. I dare to get involved." The state of Michigan is only one example:

> In a vote of 6 to 1, the Michigan State Board of Education has adopted a controversial and long-debated character education policy that includes teaching respect, responsibility, caring, trustworthiness, civic virtue, and citizenship.
>
> The policy states that "we are in the grip of a moral crisis, a crisis of individual character. The formation of character, both individual and societal, is the responsibility of all of us." The text draws from the words of Abraham Lincoln, George Washington, Martin Luther King, Jr., and other American leaders.
>
> Board President Clark Durant said he hopes schools will use the model policy to teach students about what motivated American founders. The board hopes that the four-page document will help restore civility and moral fiber to Michigan's youth.[7]

Most will agree the Michigan State Board of Education has taken a positive step. Reinforcing our nation's values with stories and quotes from the founding fathers and those who have influenced America is also a positive step, but it is only a step. Now each local school in Michigan has the choice of how to implement the new guidelines. That's where Christian parents, educators, and school board and community members must see that their voices are heard, their persuasive influence is felt, and their prayers have hands and feet. It's time to be salt, the kind that preserves and restores, not gags. It's time to volunteer your services, to speak up, encourage, and vote for those making a difference.

How to Know What Your School Values

One way to know what values your school highlights is to look at its literature program. Is your school teaching any solid, moral literature from elementary school through senior high that illustrates the highest examples of virtues and good character?

William Bennett's *Book of Virtues* is a good source. Check out titles in the school library and ask for lists of required reading at each grade level. Find out what books you can buy for your children at home or perhaps donate to your child's classroom or library.

Many years ago in this country, every part of the school curriculum reinforced biblical values, like the old *McGuffy Readers* at the turn of the century. A humorous illustration of that comes to mind. Many years ago, Virelle's mother, Virginia Fransecky, came to work at the state capital in Albany to join the Bureau of Reading Education in the New York State Education Department. She had invested much of her life in the classroom, teaching every grade but two, and had pioneered the organization of school reading centers, even writing original materials to help poor readers. Imagine her shock to learn that some of the highest reading scores in the state at that time came from a small rural school where one elderly teacher was still using the old *McGuffy Readers*. Needless to say, those reading scores made a lot of expensive programs look silly and the results were quickly hushed. But what a strong statement *that* makes about the value of a moral education coupled with great teaching.

A second barometer of your school's values is to examine what students are rewarded for at graduation, what standards of citizenship, academic excellence, leadership, and character are used? Ask to see a list of qualifications for these rewards and consider serving on a committee to institute rewards that reinforce a character education program in your school.

Is Your Character Education Program Working?

Parents with deep concerns for their children's values and moral development will recognize without any difficulty that character education in their public school in no way exempts them from the major responsibility of personally teaching their children these critical foundations to life. The schools can never, and must never, replace the authority and teaching of parents. However, schools must be held accountable for upholding the values we hold dear, as a family and collectively as a nation.

If your school already has instituted a character education program and you want to know if it's effective after the first few years, ask your administration these questions:

- Has overall academic performance improved?
- Is there less vandalism on school property?
- Are there fewer referrals to the principal's or dean's office for discipline problems?

- Has the attendance rate improved, and the drop-out rate lessened?
- What effect has there been on faculty and student morale?
- Has there been an increase in parental support of student activities and an increase in overall school spirit?
- Are the buildings and classrooms more attractive, better kept?

Many schools have shown dramatic improvements in all these areas when standards of behavior, good character, and academic performance were raised. Overall, a healthier climate for personal and academic growth is always served by higher expectations and better examples of good character.

Is it too late to turn the ship around before it heads over the falls? Should we bail out, as many have, and all climb into the lifeboats of home schooling and private schooling? That may be the only wise alternative in many cases, but sadly, it still leaves the vast majority of America's children on a doomed ship. It will take courage, faith, tenacity, and a great deal of salting influence in our local communities to right the ship, but it can be done. We need not concede the battle for our children's minds.

Chapter Highlights

- Why character education matters to Christians
- Values clarification: A giant step backward
- One community's solution: the Constitution
- Programs you can trust
- Green light: using your influence in character education curriculum choice
- Dealing with the tolerance agenda
- How to know what your school values
- How to know if your character education program is working

Key Thought

Parents with deep concerns for their children's values and moral development will recognize without any difficulty that character education in their public school in no way exempts them from the major responsibility of personally teaching their children these critical foundations to life. The schools can never, and must never, replace the authority and teaching of parents. However, schools must be held accountable for upholding the values we hold dear, as a family and collectively as a nation.

What You Can Do

1. Find out whether your local school has a values or character education program in place. If so, what values are being emphasized, and how? Who designed the curriculum? Were parents involved? How well is it working?

2. If none exists, volunteer to serve on a committee to begin such a program. Publicize it, network with other parents, invite the participation of local clergy, include teachers. Set a positive tone.

3. Contact those mentioned in the Resources section of this book who provide both curriculum and teacher training in character and values education. Begin a careful review of materials, seeking the input of other parents, teachers, and community members. Be prayerful; seek consensus.

4. For parents and children, get together and develop a list of your family's values. What matters to you? What matters to God? Discuss the many different ways these values might impact your child's school experience. Talk about the problems they may already be experiencing in living out their values. Agree to pray for one another as well as for your children's teachers.

Chapter Five

Crucial Concerns in the Classroom Understanding the Hottest Issues

Where are all the Christian people? We've stood alone too long. In the Bible, God needed only a few people to take a city, but we're too scared! **Sue Petrinec, parent**

So do not fear, for I am with you; do not be dismayed, for I am your God. I will strengthen you and help you; I will uphold you with my righteous right hand. **Isaiah 41:10**

Mark, a second grader, came home from school one day with unusual homework. "The teacher said I have to bring this back tomorrow or I can't go out on the playground. She said our moms and dads had to answer these questions. Can you help me, Mommy?"

"Sure, honey, but why don't we make it a family project after dinner? Then you can ask Daddy, too," his mom replied cheerfully. Later that evening, the "homework project" turned out to be a series of highly personal questions about their home life, level of education, and interpersonal family relationships.

"What is this and what's it for, Mark?" his dad asked. "Better yet, I'll ask your teacher myself, son." It was a pivotal moment for Mark's parents when they recognized that something other than reading, writing, and arithmetic was going on at school. It was time to get more involved.

Parents, teachers, and concerned citizens who want to "stand firm and take action," as the prophet Daniel advised, will need to know what they're talking about concerning the specific targets of everyone's complaints. We're not chasing windmills like Don Quixote; these are well-documented concerns. Here is a simple overview of the hottest issues Christian parents face with public schools, why we are so upset about them, and in some cases, what can be done.

Outcome-Based Education

The unusual assignment Mark brought home is just one wrinkle in a very large issue called outcome-based education (OBE). What does outcome-based education really mean? There are nearly as many definitions of OBE as there are people writing about it. A recent paper by Linda S. Page notes that "the most telling aspect of OBE is the failure of its proponents to agree on either a firm definition or an effective plan to implement it. OBE 'guru' Bill Spady, director of High Success Network, defines its key tenets as: success for all students; removal of the time limitation which he says traditional education requires; and an emphasis on what students will know, do, and become as opposed to what they are taught."[1] In other words, the goal becomes learning the material, or "desired outcomes," no matter how long it takes.

Why Christians Are Concerned

Quietly incorporated in these outcomes is the engineering of attitudes, tolerance of conflicting points of view, measurement of team-building ability, and other nonacademic concerns that will program students to "become" a certain type of person over time. There are striking similarities between OBE and the principles of "Total Quality Management" (TQM). As industry makes demands on educators to produce students with certain skills and behaviors, OBE and TQM are becoming quietly synonymous. This indicates the powerful synergy of business and economic demands on schooling.

The reaction of many people to OBE, including teachers, is fairly positive, or at least noncommittal, until the meaning begins to play out in nonacademic learning standards and controversial instructional techniques.

OBE is associated with some or all of the following techniques and approaches that have caused severe reactions from the Christian community:

1. Cooperative Learning
2. Higher-Order or Team Thinking
3. Experimental Programs
4. Global Education
5. Mastery Learning
6. Promoting Self-Esteem
7. Shared Decision Making
8. Teacher-as-Coach
9. Teaching Decision-Making Skills
10. Whole Language
11. Social and Emotionally Laden Learning Standards
12. Nonjudgmental Teaching and Thinking

What's Wrong with This Picture?

William Bennett put it well, "In principle it sounds good. In practice, however, OBE can be used to undermine parental authority and traditional moral and religious beliefs."[2] How does it do that? By encouraging students to believe there are no absolutes, such as right and wrong. They should think for themselves; question those in authority, both teachers and parents, and come to their own conclusions. It not only removes the standard for truth in moral areas, but also in academic areas such as reading, writing, even math, science, and history.

OBE has shown up in nearly every state plan for school improvement and largely drives Goals 2000. If local school districts, no matter how small, cannot receive funds for school improvement unless they acquiesce to national standards and adhere to very rigid requirements, this amounts to a form of social engineering that is comprehensive and consistent at both federal and state levels. The passion of the resistance to OBE is exemplified well by Phyllis Schlafly of the Eagle Forum, whose concern is that OBE is another control tactic of big government.

Two characteristics, both derived from the writings of Carl Rogers on client-centered therapy, or "nondirective counseling," are associated with OBE. Left unchecked, they will be even more insidious in their long-term effects on our children and society. They are:

- teacher as nonjudgmental facilitator
- student-centered learning

Teacher as Nonjudgmental Facilitator

In *Why Johnny Can't Tell Right from Wrong and What We Can Do About It,* William Kilpatrick notes, "For Rogers, the idea of instructing or teaching held little appeal. Instead, *Freedom to Learn* (Rogers's most influential book on education) was a guidebook for turning teachers into facilitators." Kilpatrick continues by noting that many teachers now "view their job as a therapeutic one: to facilitate self-expression, to enhance self-esteem, to be more open and nonjudgmental. In short, to be more like therapists."[3]

Student-Centered Learning

Client-centered therapy assumes meaning comes from the client, not the therapist. The same is true of student-centered learning where, similarly, meaning comes from the student, not the teacher. The teacher, then, becomes a nonjudgmental facilitator of learning, or meaning, constructed by the student. Is this confusing? Absolutely, even frightening, especially when true meaning is completely distorted by teacher-student interaction.

Who would want to have his appendix taken out by a doctor who had recreated his own meaning from his textbooks? Or who would have the courage to drive across a bridge built by someone who believed math and physics were open to his or her own self-guided meaning? Any volunteers?

There is nothing wrong with the idea of students constructing meaning, but when that meaning is obviously wrong or even dangerous, as with sex education or drug education, or any serious matter, a moral adult's perspective is critical to the student's health and well-being. Why is it so important that we know how our children are being instructed in school? Because the approaches being used can affect their worldview for life.

The Self-Esteem Movement

Included in OBE is the self-esteem movement. Seemingly innocuous, even worthy of some applause, certain aspects of the self-esteem agenda, however, aim at convincing children of an inflated personal worth apart from their eternal value as God's creation, with no standard or sense of achievement, save a rather grandiose view of themselves. Much like the story "The Emperor's New Clothes," children are led to believe they are personally dressed in greatness when, in fact, they are just beginning their life journey.

Although it is always right to affirm children for their high value as unique people, to praise their best efforts and hard work, a school's job is to help them discover their talents and begin the lifetime discipline of developing those talents to enrich others as well as themselves. Self-esteem as a byproduct of genuine achievement is one of the greatest gifts we can give children. For many children, that achievement happens in math, science, history, or English class. For others, it happens in the art room, or the music room, or on the soccer field. It can be just the boost they need.

We all remember teachers who wouldn't accept less than our best, who pushed us to perform just a little better than we had before. Virelle remembers fondly her fifth-grade teacher, Mrs. Bullock. Magnetic and bold, she was adored and feared at the same time. When Mrs. Bullock entered a classroom, she was clearly in control. No one even considered not turning in an assignment, forgetting to study for a spelling test, or offering her sloppy work. Those dark flashing eyes pierced to the soul and spoke of higher expectations than children had ever considered before, standards no decent fifth grader would dare to break! How did she look beyond the awkward country kids who filed in every morning, some still smelling of farm chores, to the capable adults they would later become—business owners, mayors, college professors, farmers, writers, caring parents? She saw the dreams in each of us and called them to life.

"Virelle, you need to enter this contest," Mrs. Bullock said as she tapped my desk with her long red fingernails and pointed to a white entry form. "It's a writing contest, and I think you could win it."

"Win it?" Virelle dared to question. I knew there were far too many fifth and sixth graders involved from several schools for me to win it. But saying no to Mrs. Bullock and not pouring my heart out to write the great American fifth-grade novel was not an option.

It was three years after my daddy had left us. I remember laboring for weeks over a story about a lost horse and a boy who loved him. The horse was, of course, my daddy. I won the contest. Even though it was fifteen years before I wrote again for the love of it, I knew the writer in me was born in Mrs. Bullock's fifth grade.

Inspiring kids to achieve more, work harder, respond positively to direction, and stretch the limits of their capabilities will do more to increase their self-esteem than any classroom sharing circle in America.

Sex Education

On the surface, sex education makes healthy sense. Leaders in the field might explain sex education as helping children develop a positive view of sexuality by providing them with information and skills about taking care of their bodies and helping them make decisions about their sexuality. Parents aren't so sure.

William Murchison, in his book *Reclaiming Morality in America*, notes: "All that sex educators can do is to clarify the mechanical details—leaving off any discussion of the mystery behind them—and wave benevolently as students leave the classroom to apply their new knowledge. No wonder sex education has so little to do with sex—that is, sex understood as the physical expression of love."[4] That's a little like explaining how a loaded gun works and then sending kids home to practice with one.

Consistent with OBE, the approaches used in sex education are nonjudgmental and devoid of moral overtones. Young people are encouraged to believe they are mature enough to handle the rising tide of sexual changes in their lives, and whatever they decide to do about it is just fine. Based on Carl Rogers's client-centered therapy, these approaches provide no room for the instructor to caution young people about the myth of safe sex, gay and lesbian sex, or to suggest that abstaining until marriage is the only perfectly safe and morally sound choice. As with drug education, the instructors serve up "a blend of facilitation, values clarification, self-esteem, and choices. Students are encouraged to question, to explore options, and to develop more tolerant attitudes toward the sexual behavior of others."[5]

Christian parents are not alone in their outrage. Parents from many differing backgrounds find it unthinkable to encourage young people to "explore options" when sexually transmitted diseases are in epidemic proportions and AIDS is rampant. To the Christian parent, sex education, or "health education" as it often ludicrously called, is frequently the last straw with the public school system. There are, however, a number of bright lights on the horizon for such parents in the form of abstinence-based curricula. Recently, fifty million dollars in annual federal funds were approved for the teaching of abstinence-based lessons. See the Resources section at the end of this book for more information on these programs.

As you approach your schools in your quest for better understanding of their sex and drug education programs, don't forget to investigate another growing issue: school-based health clinics. These clinics are currently supported by federal funding streams. Although many poor children may benefit from these clinics, there are better institutions for handling health issues than our schools. Asking schools to manage health care is really going beyond their mission. At the very least, we must bring political influence to bear on a state-by-state basis that will limit the range of services these health clinics provide. But don't be surprised when you hear of the "schoolhome" of the future. It may be closer to reality than you think.

On a more positive note, for four years Virelle worked in our local elementary school assisting several fourth- and fifth-grade teachers with their reading and writing programs. She enjoyed it immensely and found many of the teachers there exemplary. During that time, the annual fifth-grade "Health Curriculum" was taught. It was a video lesson on the changes to expect in ten-year-old bodies during puberty, one video for boys and one for girls. The boys' class was led by a male teacher, and the girls' class by a female teacher and Virelle!

At first she was apprehensive, but ended up with a new appreciation for the difficulties public school teachers face as they handle these duties. She learned that the curriculum may be "safe" and inoffensive, but the questions the kids ask are not. Her little class of fifth-grade girls asked about things Virelle had never heard of until college, and sometimes not even then! She marveled at the tact and diplomacy that was used to field these questions by several highly moral and wonderful teachers. They deserve our applause. We hope the same is true in your district.

School Prayer

At a time when many of today's Baby Boomers were buying prom gowns and working on college applications, a radical change was happening to their alma maters. God was being systematically ushered out the school door. Things have never been the same since.

Gone are the days many of us remember fondly when our public school principal read a passage of Scripture every morning before giving the day's announcements. Gone are the framed Ten Commandments and the Golden Rule that gave teachers great respect and authority in their students' eyes and kept more than one of us on the straight and narrow. Gone are the moving Christmas pageants, the prayers before assemblies, and the sense of school as a valued instrument God used to build character and shape and direct lives.

David Barton summarizes the change in his booklet *"What Happened in Education?"* as follows:

> 1963—Religious Principles Prohibited in Schools. As a result of Supreme Court decisions in *Engel v. Vitale, Murray v. Curlett,* and *Abington v. Schempp,* religious principles were separated from public education. School prayer, Bible reading, and any instruction which purported to have any type of religious connection were all prohibited in schools. So thorough was the eradication of these principles that even the Ten Commandments, acknowledged by the Court to be the basis of law in the Western World, were eventually removed from schools. The traditional basis for any absolutes concerning right and wrong in behavior, belief, and conduct were withdrawn from educational instruction and philosophy.[6]

Even if every Congressman or woman in Washington decided to undo the damage tomorrow, how would they begin? Although most Americans support school prayer, we don't want teachers and students reciting acceptable state prayers, nor do we want them censored for praying quietly by themselves or in a small group in school.

Eleven of the top conservative Christian groups came together to discuss these issues. In the May 1995 "Focus on the Family Newsletter" they concluded: "The problem is broader than prayer in the schools. We are faced with an assault on religious liberties at many levels, and any effort to remedy it should be aimed at the wider issue."[7]

For a more comprehensive look at school prayer and the current status of legislation on religious freedoms, we recommend sending for a copy of this newsletter and the up-to-date information on current legislation that will surely be available to you. Even though some may not consider school prayer an extremely controversial issue, decisions made in this area will affect tomorrow's leaders who are in school today.

A Mixed Bag: Multiculturalism, Eco-Education, and Homosexuality

It is nearly beyond comprehension that these issues have been included in school curricula. Expecting schools to do a good job teaching classic core subjects and bring students to higher levels of achievement is challenge enough. But to pile on their backs the agendas of special-interest groups representing homosexuality, multicultural education, and the diverse learning styles of all ethnic groups puts an impossible burden on all but a few schools. Why are these concerns controversial, and what effect might they have on students?

Multicultural Education

Multicutural education basically means designing programs to increase cultural sensitivity and accommodate the specific learning styles of children from various ethnic groups, including but not limited to African-Americans, Asian Americans, Hispanic Americans, and Native Americans. It began in the 1960s as a good idea: Help children from other language and cultural backgrounds to learn better and help others understand and appreciate them better. However, it soon became a major divider of citizens along the lines of race and culture. As Diane Ravitch, an educational policy analyst, noted, "The most strident critics of the common culture demand that the curriculum teach contempt for the founders of the nation and for everything European or white."[8] This has been and will continue to be a heated issue.

Rita Dunn, director of the Center for the Study of Learning and Teaching at St. John's University, came to this conclusion:

> The research [Dunn and Griggs 1995] clearly shows that there is no such thing as a cultural group [learning] style. There are cross-cultural and intracultural similarities and differences among all peoples. Those differences are enriching when understood and channeled positively.
>
> Given this information, I believe it is unwise for schools with limited budgets to support multicultural education in addition to—and apart from—regular education. . . . The melting pot concept does not diminish one's heritage. It unites the strengths of many cultures into a single, stronger blend of culture to reflect the best of all.[9]

Rather than a celebration of children's heritage, multicultural education separates and divides us and has little to do with helping kids learn.

Eco-Education

Eco-education is not bad in and of itself, but why can't it be taught within traditional science courses? It has garnered its own place in the curriculum with little justification. Environmental education tries to sensitize students to the natural world and how badly humans are treating it. The concern comes when schools use sensational materials designed to make students react negatively to every invention of man that might affect the environment. Paying attention to the environment and the quality of air and water every day is important. Spending inordinate amounts of instructional time studying the environment, and planting fear in children, is inappropriate in the K-12 curriculum. Make sure your schools are not using shock techniques to make children feel the world is coming to an end because of pollution or openings in the ozone layer!

Homosexuality

This is now a part of our everyday world. Marches, TV specials, gay and lesbian "proms" in high school, and gay marriages are just a few of the events we are exposed to much more frequently than in the near past. Being kind and loving to people of all persuasions and lifestyles is biblical. Supporting, condoning, and advocating perversion is wrong. If schools invite gay and lesbian speakers in to talk with students, why not invite moms and dads in to talk about the joys of wholesome sexuality and family life? School districts, afraid of lawsuits from the burgeoning ranks of gay and lesbian political activists, are bending over backwards to be tolerant of every special-interest group that speaks up or petitions the board for a hearing. Advocating diverse lifestyles should not be part of the school curriculum.

Phonics Vs. Whole Language

An experienced teacher whose district had bought the whole-language approach whole hog concluded, "I'm definitely more 'half language' than 'whole language.'" Given the wide range of abilities and learning styles in her elementary school classroom, she recognized that highly verbal students learn well with many varieties of instruction, but average or below-average students can struggle badly when only offered a whole-language approach. They are unable to "fill in the gaps" of correct grammar, spelling, and the phonetic understanding of language and meaning without a great deal of outside help.

When our oldest daughter entered her freshman year at Cornell University, she was accustomed to a rigorous academic schedule. Her grades in high school were admirably high. Imagine her shock, and ours, when she failed the preliminary English grammar exam her first month in college!

"I never learned this in high school," she moaned over the phone. "I must have been absent the day they taught grammar!"

"What do you mean the *day* they taught grammar?" Virelle, a former English major, countered, "Nobody can teach grammar in a day! It's taught gradually in small bites all throughout school. You mean you never learned *any* grammar? How is that possible?" Sadly, a call to the high school language arts department confirmed the ugly truth: The study of grammar had been discarded from the curriculum several years before. Kids were now expected to derive, or somehow absorb, the correct use of English from reading and writing. How had we allowed that to happen?

As extreme as it is to base an entire language arts curriculum solely on a child's own selection of literature and a loosely structured writing program, it can be just as extreme to return to a more rigid, basal reader system. The one saving grace of whole language is that children are learning to love reading once again and to write with more freedom of expression and a greater emphasis on meaning. The very best teachers will savor the strengths of both phonics and whole language. They will not neglect the symmetry and beauty of the correct use of the English language, the appreciation of well-chosen, morally based literature, and the disciplines of good writing, but in doing so, they will pull out every stop to encourage a love of reading and writing and a creative, yet responsible, use of classroom time. They will be, in effect, "half-language" too.

Creation and Evolution

Christian teachers like Laura Johnson, whose story is told in chapter 11, have found creative ways to teach evolution as simply a theory and the credibility of creation as an equally viable theory that deserves honest examination. She urges her eighth-grade students not to just accept evolution as a scientific fact, but to recognize their own value as human beings based on how they came to be or who made them. Although public school classrooms have become notoriously anti-faith in their assertion of evolution as scientific fact, Christian students and parents can still maintain a voice and have an impact through open debate, guest expert speakers, and the request for equal time to explain the reasonable, credible, scientific evidence for creation.

Block Scheduling

Block scheduling, or semestering, is a reorganization of the school day into several ninety-minute segments that cover in a half-year the same academic ground once covered in a full-year course of fifty-minute classes. The idea is that longer classes allow for a more relaxed pace, different styles of teaching, and more in-depth treatment of subjects. Early research is showing that there are problems with this approach related to retention, attention span, and overall performance. (For more in-depth information refer to web site: http://www.athenet.net/~jlindsay/Block.shtml#intro.)

We're in a sound byte world. Today's video babies have been raised on thirty-second information slots. Even if it is more relaxed and pleasant, expecting them to stay focused and attentive for ninety-minute time slots is a big stretch to their adolescent attention spans. When shorter courses rather than year-long courses are taught by teachers who may not have been trained how to use two-hour time blocks, kids are often exhausted, retain less information, and end up wasting time. If your school is considering block scheduling, or semestering, refer them to the web site mentioned above, noting particularly the Canadian research on the negative effect block scheduling has on student performance.

Internet Use

From elementary grades through high school, schools are loaded with technology and there's more to come. Today's kids are techno-geniuses, computer whizzes who flash like lightning from the Internet to CD-Roms to word processing, while their teachers often stand and watch, jaws dropped in amazement. Teachers need training as do volunteers from the community to allow students greater use of technology without the compromise of instructional time or individual attention.

Good ways to use the Internet include worldwide collaborative projects on scientific investigations that allow students to interact with scientists, international pen pals, research, etc. Bad ways are common: Sending kids to the library or computer center with little or no training and giving them access to the entire Internet, allowing them to do "cheap research" by simply reformatting printed information on a given topic. Schools might do well to require students to "log on" to Internet time and keep a diary of how they use their time.

Questions to Ask Your School About Internet Use

- Is there a written policy on Internet use by students?
- Is the software being used to access the Internet, especially at the elementary level, pre-programmed to web sites that are safe for kids?
- Have teachers been given proper training through staff development on the best uses of the Internet?

Computers are marvelous tools, but they can't replace a teacher. Used well, they open vast storehouses of knowledge and interactive learning. Supervised carelessly, they can be a nonproductive or even a destructive waste of time.

Portfolio Assessment

Portfolio assessment is the collection of materials organized chronologically over a student's school career that provide a more in-depth and personal picture of that student's progress rather than simply relying on standardized or local test scores for evaluation. It should include dated work samples, interviews, observations, inventories, screening test results, and any information that is relevant about the progress of that child.

The strengths of portfolio assessment are that a child's best work from each area is chosen, as in a writing or art portfolio, showing their developing talents and abilities over long blocks of time. The weaknesses occur when used without the benefit of equally important academic measurements and test scores, in which case a portfolio presents an incomplete, or even a biased, picture. Since a child's progress is compared only with himself, it makes it difficult for parents to know how their child is doing academically among his peers. Portfolio assessment is an incomplete, though valuable, tool for assessing student progress. It can never replace grades and more clear-cut evaluations of academic goals.

School Safety

We've come a long way from the days when a trip to the principal's office made students quake in their shoes, as afraid of the principal as they were at having Mom or Dad find out what they did. Steve has often visited the locked environments of inner city schools where teachers commonly carry brass knuckles and even young students are trained to "hit the floor" under their desks at the *pop! pop! pop!* of gunfire outside.

Violence toward teachers and fellow students in suburban schools is not uncommon today. Neither are drug-sniffing police dogs, metal detectors, or undercover cops. What's happened in American schools to allow such violence to take control?

The erosion of the family has produced a new generation of youth with less and less respect for authority. Second, schools have lost the legal power and community backing to discipline offenders. We hear of crazy lawsuits every day where football players who have been kicked off the team and suspended from school for drunkenness or vandalism are let back on within a week because their parents sued the school and won. What message does this give younger children?

Local law enforcement agencies, school administrators, and PTAs need to adopt strict discipline policies for their individual communities. One solution is to create a contract for students and parents to sign to allow them the continued privilege of a public education. Discipline practices can be agreed on long before the problem arises, and educators must be given the authority to suspend and expel students who endanger others, break school rules, or are rude and disrespectful to teachers. Included in school discipline should be standards of decency for language and dress. It's time we tightened up the school environment and the use of tax dollars and protect the classroom from those who are violent, offensive, and blatantly disrespectful.

How can we as parents, educators, and community members help our schools stay focused on their mission: to equip students with the intellectual tools necessary to enter this complex adult world, to discover and develop their God-given gifts and talents, to become lifelong learners who regularly visit the storehouses of knowledge, art, great literature, the richness and wisdom of history, the intricacies of math and science? We must serve more as mentors and coaches than critics. When given the opportunity, we must speak with clarity and conviction, but above all, we must not give up.

Chapter Highlights

- Outcome-based education
- Teacher as nonjudgmental facilitator
- Student-centered learning
- The self-esteem movement
- Sex education
- School prayer
- A mixed bag: multiculturalism, eco-education, and homosexuality
- Phonics vs. whole language
- Creation and evolution
- Block scheduling
- Internet use
- Portfolio assessment
- School safety

Key Thought

Parents, teachers, and concerned citizens who want to "stand firm and take action" as the prophet Daniel advised will need to know what they're talking about concerning the specific targets of everyone's complaints. We're not chasing windmills like Don Quixote; these are well-documented concerns.

What You Can Do

1. Consider organizing a group of concerned parents, and discuss the above-mentioned issues to determine which issues are currently affecting your local school system.
2. Gather more information on specific issues. Check the Internet for related articles, refer to local experts if available, and check your library.
3. Check the listing of resources at the end of this book for listings of current information. Make certain you are on their regular mailing lists.
4. Make an appointment, along with at least one other concerned individual, to visit your school administrator or curriculum specialist. Ask about their policies on these issues and how your views can, or are, being considered. Contact several board members and your district representative on the state legislature to inform them of your concerns.
5. For parents, talk with your children every day about what happens in school. Listen carefully. It may take children a while to bring up discussions or lessons in school that disturb them. Ask questions carefully, pray about it together, and ask God to help you guide them wisely.

Chapter Six

Education 101 The Seven Building Blocks of Schooling

A free education was intended to educate individuals to participate in a democratic society. We cannot fail to try to do this. There are so many children than can be helped even by one-on-one interaction. We must continue to be a part of the process of public education. **Jean G. Burns, retired teacher and supervisor of student teachers**

The wise in heart are called discerning, and pleasant words
promote instruction. **Proverbs 16:21**

Welcome to Eastside Elementary School! Once

inside the door, expect to be greeted by a small, energetic man with a strong handshake and big smile. Dr. Hewitt has been principal for longer than most families have even lived in his community. In fact, many of the parents he's greeting today were once little kids who hopped off the school bus and found him there every morning and every afternoon addressing them by name, asking how well they learned their math facts, or congratulating them for the beautiful mural they helped to paint in their classroom.

Not everyone has loved Dr. Hewitt over the years. Teachers who screamed at their students and tore up their papers received "walking papers" of their own when the spring contracts came out. Disrespectful children who frequented his office for class discipline problems didn't like him much, nor did those who mistreated any of the handicapped students who enjoyed Eastside's special education program. Dr. Hewitt insisted on absolute respect for teachers, for the rights and feelings of fellow students, and especially for traditional values our country has held dear for generations.

Flag Day was a big event at Eastside Elementary. The parking lot was jammed with parents' cars, many dads and moms taking time away from work at office and home to watch the whole school march in serious procession, class flag bearer in front, around the flagpole green. The fourth- and fifth-grade band tooted "America the Beautiful" and a few simplified Sousa marches, ending with the Pledge of Allegiance and "The Star Spangled Banner." The best essays on "What the Flag Means to Me" were read by students from each grade in front of the whole school. There were few dry eyes.

Even as the Christmas season became the "holidays" at schools across America, Eastside spilled over with music honoring Hanukkah, Christmas, snowmen, and reindeer. Beneath a large Christmas tree in the front entrance hall, decorated with beaming Polaroid grins, the music teacher sat at a small piano and played the entire week before vacation, stopping once each hour to direct classes of singers whose teacher led them down to serenade the school, or just to grab a cup of hot chocolate and a few cookies.

What parent can forget the pride his children felt earning achievement awards, publishing a composition in the school paper, or performing in one of Eastside's many concerts and student-written theater productions? What was it about this school that attracted parent volunteers like a magnet, boasted some of the highest reading and math scores in the state, and helped children learn to reach for the best in their own talents and abilities?

Well-run schools are great places to visit and exciting environments for children. They are effective for many reasons, including highly competent principals and teachers. Their effectiveness is shown in the healthy academic, social, physical, and emotional progress of their students, the high morale of the faculty, consistent support and involvement of parents as well as a solid record of overall school achievement. It doesn't happen by chance. At Eastside Elementary the seven building blocks of schooling are carefully aligned, regularly reviewed, continually evaluated. Schools simply don't improve without them.

As you talk with the leadership of your public school, both teachers and principals should be able to tell you how your school lines up in these seven critical areas:

Seven Building Blocks of Schooling

1. Worldview and beliefs
2. Learning standards
3. Learning theory
4. Curriculum
5. Assessment
6. Alignment
7. Accountability

Every school needs a solid foundation to become a strong and healthy learning environment. Like the foundation of a great building, each of these blocks builds on the previous one. The choice of learning standards is conditioned by worldview and beliefs. Learning standards set the stage for the type of learning theory and appropriate curricula the school chooses, including the instructional approach used. The assessment of student achievement will be aligned with learning theory and the curriculum. This approach makes sure what is tested has actually been taught. Accountability includes public reports on all aspects of schooling, from finances to student suspensions and achievement, and provides a strong information base for improving school results.

Of course, there are other important characteristics of schooling that contribute significantly to success. They relate more subtly to school culture and include the quality of leadership (you'll learn about this whenever you talk with teachers), the teachers' love for their students and subjects, and the tone of the entire school learning climate, including the two "new Rs," respect and responsibility. However, without a solid foundation, school improvement will be shaky and sporadic.

Once we grasp the importance of these seven building blocks of schooling, we are better equipped to begin a constructive, well-informed conversation with our local school system and more quickly discern areas of weakness. Let's take a look at each one.

1. Worldview and Beliefs

Once we know a person's worldview, we can explain most of their actions and even predict many of their decisions. A person's worldview is the lens through which he interprets life, its origin, significance, and purpose.[1] David A. Noebel, a Christian philosopher, explains worldview in his extensive work, *Understanding the Times*:

The term *worldview* refers to any ideology, philosophy, theology, movement, or religion that provides an overarching approach to understanding God, the world, and man's relations to God and the world. Specifically, a worldview should contain a particular perspective regarding each of the following ten disciplines: theology, philosophy, ethics, biology, psychology, sociology, law, politics, economics, and history.[2]

Worldview is part of the foundation of schooling, but it is often unstated or unwritten. It's easy to see why it's important, because the worldview of those who choose the curriculum will affect which subjects are taught. A teacher's worldview will affect the way they are taught. A principal's and superintendent's worldviews determine which values and standards will define the school climate and influence their decisions.

Most educators and board members will be uncomfortable with the question of worldview, but to some degree it still must be pursued. Communities need to know whether their educators' worldviews are secular humanism or Judeo-Christian, why they make certain decisions, and whether they will uphold agreed-on moral values and standards of character in their schools. Although worldview is usually part of the "hidden curriculum" in most school districts, it needs to be more explicit and out in the open.

One way parents and school districts have dealt with this issue is through mission, vision, and belief statements. The following belief statement from the Corning City School District in New York is one illustration:

WE BELIEVE:

1. The community is responsible for maintaining an environment conducive to learning.

2. Home and family experiences strongly affect student learning.

3. Cooperation between home and school is critical to student success.

4. Teachers and students have a shared responsibility for learning.

5. All school district staff are responsible for providing and maintaining an environment that supports the teaching/learning process.

6. Change cannot occur without risk taking.

7. We can achieve excellence.

8. All students can learn.

9. All individuals have value.

10. Schools must be safe and secure.

11. All students should have equal opportunities for educational experiences.

12. Education is a lifelong process.

13. Education is essential to a democratic society.

14. The entire focus of the educational process centers on what's best for students.[3]

You can see from this example that a basic philosophy of education is taking shape, but there are glaring gaps that prevent us from understanding their worldview. There is a strong emphasis on the home-school connection, but little or no evidence to clarify a Judeo-Christian worldview. Also missing is any mention of the development of character or moral values such as honesty, respect, fairness, self-discipline, responsibility, tolerance, or cooperation.

Now look at a belief statement from Central Square Central School District, Central Square, New York, with a greater emphasis on moral values:

WE BELIEVE:

1. Lifelong learning is essential to maintain and improve the quality of life.

2. Community benefits when the talents of all its members are nurtured and shared.

3. All individuals are accountable for the actions they decide to take.

4. All individuals are role models, and positive role models are essential for the community's prosperity.

5. Everyone can learn, but at different rates and in different ways.

6. Positive attitudes toward self, others, and one's surroundings lead to positive outcomes.

7. Open, honest, and ongoing communication within the community is essential for trust, understanding, and cooperation.

8. Integrity is the most important human quality.[4]

This may not quite meet the standard you'd like to see, but most of us will find it a vast improvement. As you can imagine, mission and belief statements involve a major community effort. It's a perfect place for Christians to make a lasting impact.

Those who think we're making too much of worldview and beliefs may think differently after reading what John J. Dunphy, a true humanist, writes about schools and Christians in *The Humanist Magazine*:

> I am convinced that the battle for humankind's future must be waged and won in the public school classroom by teachers [who] correctly perceive their role as proselytizers of a new faith which will replace the rotting corpse of Christianity.[5]

That sums up the true secular humanist's concern for education, social engineering, and reverence for God. And it doesn't end there.

There are educational change models driven by those opposed to biblical Christianity who would redesign our schools according to a worldview that includes a type of New Age spirituality. If a child's mind is filled with these types of learning activities every day for thirteen or more years, students will graduate with knowledge, skills, and attitudes that may differ radically from what parents expected. They may even become quite comfortable in a New Age culture. It simply makes sense to insist that our public schools operate in agreement with the worldview and values of the parents and taxpayers who support them.

2. Learning Standards

In raising standards for student achievement, a great deal of effort is being placed on specifying the highest level of achievement possible in all subjects for all students. Learning standards typically have two components:

1. content standards, which describe what students should know or be able to do at different points in their education; and
2. performance standards, which describe how well they should be able to do it.

States have been developing higher standards for about ten years. The best way to develop them is through a combination of expertise, review by teachers, and approval by representative community members throughout a state.

It is important that learning standards be established before state assessment systems are redesigned to measure student achievement of those standards. Valid and reliable measures of student achievement take time and money to develop.

School districts develop their own learning standards or goals and then design curriculum and assessment around these goals. If the state has performance exams that measure state level learning standards, school districts are careful to create learning

---

Examples of Learning Standards

Missouri, Science Standard: "In Science, students in Missouri public schools will acquire a solid foundation which includes knowledge of properties and principles of force and motion."[6]

Oregon, Grades 6–8 Reading Standard and Benchmark: "Demonstrate inferential comprehension of a variety of printed materials." Associated Grade 8 Benchmark: "Identify relationships, images, patterns or symbols and draw conclusions about their meaning."[7]

New York, Mathematics, Science, and Technology Standard 1, Analysis, Inquiry, and Design: "Students will use mathematical analysis, scientific inquiry, and engineering design, as appropriate, to pose questions, seek answers, and develop solutions."[8]

---

goals that will help their students do very well on these state tests. If no state tests are administered, school districts can design curriculum and assessments around their own learning goals.

Basically, the tighter the relationships among learning standards, curriculum, instruction, and assessment, the easier it is for school districts to monitor changes in strategies and improvements in student achievement.

3. Learning Theory

Learning theory is important to schooling. It isn't discussed with parents and is seldom discussed with teachers, but the way teachers think about learning drastically affects instruction and assessment.

Learning is many things to many people. The following types of learning are probably used by most teachers:

- conditioning,
- processing information, and
- constructing knowledge.

Conditioning

Remember Pavlov's dogs that learned to salivate at the sound of a bell? That's how most of us learn about life: the hard way. It's called *conditioning,* and it goes back to the theories developed by learning psychologist B. F. Skinner. Conditioning occurs when a child touches a hot object and a parent or teacher yells, "No, don't touch that!" When he gets burned, the child learns that next time it's better to heed words of warning and avoid the pain. Conditioning is an important type of learning, because it can occur quickly and requires little deep thinking.

Punishment is related to conditioning when pain or suffering follows a student's actions. If you were taught in a Catholic school twenty-five or thirty years ago, you get the point. Today, very little if any punishing is done in public schools.

Positive reinforcement is also a type of conditioning that is used heavily in schooling. Positive reinforcement is the use of rewards such as praise, appropriate touch—hugs, celebration, positive letters sent home, high grades, treats, time on the playground, etc. Rewards are endless in type and frequency, and most teachers use them. However, rewards are external and can become manipulative, so caution is necessary. Great teachers know how to use the right rewards with individual students. It's an art, not a science.

Processing Information

Processing information occurs, for example, in a math class when the teacher puts a problem on the chalkboard or computer screen, demonstrates how to solve it, and then gives students nearly identical problems to solve in the same fashion. The teacher "transmits" information directly to the student, who processes that information, hopefully in the same way the teacher does.

This approach to learning works with some students whose minds operate in ways similar to their teacher's, but for students "responding to a different drummer," big trouble is in store. The "sage on the stage" who lectures a lot, transmitting content, also puts many of them to sleep. All students simply do not learn things the same way. The best teachers have learned to vary instruction accordingly.

Constructing Knowledge

One of the most amazing things about the human mind is its ability to anticipate. The mind is always "reaching forward." God made our minds to be computer-like, "sense-making" machines, for lack of a better metaphor.

The simple truth is, no matter what someone is teaching, you'll never learn anything if you're not thinking. But what is thinking?

Constructing knowledge is a broad description of how individuals learn. Piaget, the famous Swiss biologist who became a psychologist, was a "constructivist" who believed that the mind actually "works on" information coming into it and transforms it into meaning for each individual. Sometimes the information it receives is processed and understood very efficiently; other times, great mental adjustment is needed before the mind comes back into balance and can continue thinking clearly. In this way, the mind continually acts on incoming information and makes sense of it. That's the beginning of thinking.

Learning is a consequence of thinking, and thinking is the formation of ideas or concepts in the mind that help us deal with our "inner" and our "outer" worlds. Some of us do our best thinking in the shower or on a long walk.

What do you think is the best way to improve thinking and, therefore, enhance learning? Should students memorize everything or learn things only in context? Can students come to a rich understanding of a topic without explaining their ideas to others? Both thinking and learning rest in the strength of language skills and in regular practice. Reading, writing, listening, and speaking lead to improvement in every subject area.

"Language is the dress of thought," said Samuel Johnson, eighteenth-century satirist.[9] Human beings were designed to learn through language. (Reflect for a moment on the beginning of John's Gospel, "And the Word became flesh and dwelt among us.") Any theory of learning and instruction that does not emphasize the role of language falls far short.

Do you want your children to become independent thinkers capable of expressing themselves well, justifying their answers under pressure? Or do you want them to simply memorize everything and parrot it back or just answer multiple-choice questions well? The type of thinker, writer, or speaker you want students to become will depend on how they are taught and tested. The type of person you want students to become will depend on the character and integrity of those doing the teaching.

The current trend in learning theory has been developing for more than fifty years. It is called constructivism. Learners construct larger concepts based on their experiences and understandings. To some degree, it shows respect for the knowledge kids bring to school, but at the same time, it's much different than the information-processing model, which expects students to learn specific information and explain what they've learned.

4. Curriculum

Curriculum is the road map teachers use for the year's learning activities in their particular discipline. It outlines the academic ground to be covered and holds schools

Red Flag: Constructivism

Heated debates surround all aspects of this theoretical perspective. There are knowledgeable researchers who are completely amazed that constructivism is applied so broadly to learning and instruction.

Constructivism can mean many things to people and should be viewed with skepticism, especially if your school district has bought into it and is trying to apply it to instruction and assessment.[10] (See endnotes for even more upsetting information on radical constructivism.)

The bottom line is: Don't let anyone in your school district bring up the word *constructivism* without a detailed explanation. And it will come up: New York State's entire vision of Learning-Centered Curriculum is based on constructivism.[11] There are many faces to this theory; not all are bad, but its philosophical underpinnings can be far from a Judeo-Christian worldview. Christians know where their information comes from. Most constructivists don't care.

on course. Teachers should be able to hand you a copy of their curriculum and show you exactly where they are in it. Each curriculum for a course of study should include:

- the arrangements a school makes for students' learning and development, including sequence, format, and content;
- student activities;
- teaching approaches;
- books, materials, and resources used; and
- the way teachers and classes are organized to maximize effectiveness.

State learning standards can be very explicit and should be considered as schools design local curriculum guides. One strong reason for this is state tests. If the highest-level diplomas in your state are based on student performance on state tests, then not following those learning standards could prevent students from receiving state-sanctioned diplomas.

The flip side of higher state standards is more control. If a state sets the learning standards and emphasizes an approach to learning that lends itself to very prescriptive guidelines, syllabi, and tests, the state could go all the way with mandating all aspects of the local curriculum. This happens in some other countries. It was once said of France that on any given day of the school year at 10:00 A.M., all students throughout France would be studying algebra! That's a controlling educational system!

Curriculum design includes things such as course content, choice of textbooks, and teaching technique, even the impact of teachers on students. It can also include explicit directions to teach accepted moral values throughout all subjects. It's a serious issue today as textbooks, for example on American history, are being used that bear little resemblance to the traditional course of study most of us learned. Imagine graduating high school seniors who have never studied the Declaration of Independence, the Constitution and the ideals of the Founding Fathers, Lincoln's Gettysburg Address and the grief and passion of the Civil War, or America's emerging role in world leadership, and our part in the great world wars.

Designing curriculum is a powerful and positive way to influence the future of this nation. Find out what part you can play in your own school district and offer your services on textbook and curriculum development committees.

5. Assessment

Assessment (measuring, reporting, and reflecting on student accomplishment) is a critical part of what makes schools tick. People always pay attention to what is tested or measured, whether in the office, on the factory floor, or in the school. Assessment is a barometer of your school's success in educating your children.

There is less testing today using the old true-false, fill-in-the-blank, and multiple-choice tests. Instead, there is greater emphasis on process-oriented measurement of student achievement over longer periods of time in an attempt to capture the richness of student accomplishment. It's called performance assessment.

Changes in assessment are occurring at the same time that large-scale educational reform models are being implemented. This is definitely causing confusion at the local level because state leadership in assessment is lagging behind changes in curriculum and instruction. If it weren't for increases in teacher training and staff development in these areas, our educational system would be in even deeper trouble.

Current debates over national testing in elementary level reading and math aren't all bad. Some states fall far behind others and their children suffer. National testing could help bring all states up to par.

6. Alignment

Driving a car without the wheels in alignment produces a bumpy ride. Likewise, the alignment of learning standards and theory with curriculum, instruction, and assessment is pivotal to educational excellence. Higher learning standards and learning theory need to be aligned with instructional practice and assessment techniques. Appropriate assessment will tell teachers and parents if students are achieving the standards.

In their book, *Assessing Student Outcomes: Performance Assessment Using the Dimensions of Learning Model,* Robert Marzano, Debra Pickering, and Jay McTighe summarize the importance of alignment:

> [I]f we want students to engage in complex tasks in which they will use knowledge in unique and meaningful ways . . . and if we want them to cultivate such higher level mental skills as restraining impulsivity and being aware of their own thinking . . . , then our methods of assessment must surely change, because most of today's assessments make no attempt to measure such behaviors; they are not linked to the kind of learning we want to see. Likewise, the nature and delivery of curriculum must change to become more strongly linked to learning and assessment.[12]

Hopefully, learning standards, instruction, and assessment will be aligned at state and local levels so that school improvement can be evaluated and schools can be held accountable for the achievement of all students, regardless of background.

7. Accountability: How Does Your School Measure Up?

The monitoring of school performance is undergoing radical changes. States are holding local school districts more accountable than in the past. In the area of finances, more school districts are being audited to make sure they are spending money according to both state and federal regulations. Comprehensive reporting systems are being designed to gauge school quality. These new accountability systems and public reporting requirements will help communities determine school effectiveness and efficiency.

School reports on student achievement are also becoming more sophisticated, meaningful, and helpful. Information on student achievement is being reported by gender and ethnicity—Caucasian, Black, Hispanic, Native American. These breakdowns help everyone see whether a school's programs are having the same effect across these groups. When discrepancies are found, targeted action can take place to improve student achievement.

Another helpful type of reporting indicates how well students are doing compared to students in similar communities with similar per-pupil expenditures. In addition to student achievement measures in core subjects at selected grades, schools are also reporting attendance, suspension, and dropout rates.

States usually allow schools to operate as long as they meet registration requirements. Traditionally, school registration requirements included fiscal accountability, health and safety requirements, and building and fire code standards. Now, student achievement is often tied to registration status. When schools don't meet these requirements, progressive sanctions are initiated. These sanctions include giving school districts three years to improve conditions in the buildings, student achievement, attendance rate, suspension and dropout rates. If these sanctions don't work, the local superintendent can be removed and a state-appointed manager and advisory board put in place to develop new school improvement plans.

The Heart of Schooling

These seven building blocks of schooling round out the culture of learning in your school. They form the heart of schooling and reflect its culture. This culture can easily vary from building to building within the same district due to leadership style, teacher quality, parent participation, and commitment.

Remember that ultimately school reform can begin or end when teachers close their classroom doors. Teachers are central to the improvement of our schools. Good teachers deserve our respect and appreciation. Most of them will welcome your interest and gladly work with you to improve schooling.

As our school improvement efforts increase, so will the level of our communication with teachers and school officials. When the words we use to talk about schooling, however, are too combative, increased polarization over issues weakens our effectiveness. We tend to use military terms like "lining up" on the "right" side of controversies and planning our next "strategy." If we truly desire better schools, we'll need to turn the conversation to one of purpose and possibility, not constant, crushing criticism.

The words we use with schools should be clear and positive. Mike Rose, a professor at UCLA's graduate school of education, has a special way of expressing the significance of the *public* words we use to try to improve our schools:

> Safety, respect, expectation, opportunity, vitality, the intersection of heart and mind, the creation of civic space—this should be our public vocabulary of schooling—for that fact, of a number of our public institutions.[13]

Carefully chosen, measured language goes a long way toward improving relationships with school leaders and teachers. Having a better understanding of these seven building blocks of schooling will give you more confidence and help you be better equipped to understand local-school culture and to bring about healthy change.

Chapter Highlights

Seven building blocks of schooling:

- Worldview and beliefs
- Learning standards
- Learning theory
- Curriculum
- Assessment
- Alignment
- Accountability

Key Thought

Well-run schools are great places to visit and exciting environments for children. They are effective for many reasons, including highly competent principals and teachers. Their effectiveness is shown in the healthy academic, social, physical, and emotional progress of their students, the high morale of the faculty, consistent support and involvement of parents as well as a solid record of overall school achievement. It doesn't happen by chance.

What You Can Do

1. Contact five school districts in your region and compare the following factors:
   - student achievement on standardized tests and state tests,
   - achievement differences by gender and ethnicity,
   - drop out rate, suspension rate, and attendance rate, and
   - per-pupil expenditure.

   Notice how your school district compares with others.
2. Based on this information, choose the area of greatest concern in your district and find out what, if anything, is being done to make improvements. Contact members of the board of education and communicate your findings to them. Look for ways to help your district move toward positive change.

3. If there is a concept or term being used by your school with which you are unfamiliar, such as *constructivism*, ask your principal, curriculum coordinator, or superintendent what it means and how it is being used. Is there any assessment of its effectiveness?

Chapter Seven

How School Districts Work Control and Influence at the Local Level

In our school the most involved parents are Mormons. We value the time they have given to the classrooms and school, but I would like to see the Christian parents give as much time and energy as they do, serving on the board, the PTA, and the School Site Council, for example. **Ginny Edwards, teacher**

Remind the people to be subject to rulers and authorities, to be obedient, to be ready to do whatever is good, to slander no one, to be peaceable and considerate, and to show true humility toward all men.
Titus 3:1–2

No one was surprised when the voters in a small rural school district voted down a proposed 38 percent increase in their local taxes. Granted, money was needed to fund major building improvements at the middle school and high school, but no one expected the bill to be so high. Hadn't the school board promised that nearly all the money would come from state funding? Senior citizens worried about losing their homes. Some gave up and sold them prematurely.

Even after trimming school programs, a huge gap remained between building costs and what the community could afford. Everyone assumed the project would be scaled back or delayed, but construction began anyway. The board of education, with the approval of the superintendent of schools, adopted a contingency budget without taxpayer approval, and began the $68.5 million project over the summer, locking homeowners into a 10.9 percent increase in taxes with more to come. When schools were scheduled to open in September, the buildings weren't ready on time, and both students and teachers waited an extra week at home. No one was happy.

It's a common story, not unlike the dissent and polarization that accompany raised taxes, costly increases, and closed-door board meetings in many communities across America, including our own. As great as the needs may be for additional classrooms, improved school libraries, updated bathrooms and buses, school officials often appear with a trump card for getting things done at the taxpayers' expense. How does this happen?

To learn how, we have to understand first how things work behind the scenes, not just in financial areas, but in nitty-gritty decision making at every level.

Who Controls the Purse Strings?

Who has the greatest control and influence on how money is going to be spent and on which programs will operate in your district? Politics and influence often determine which programs get the most money. Recently, this has been true of money for technology in schools. Programs that get the most money may also be driven by particular philosophies of education that may not be compatible with your community's vision for education or your worldview. When millions of dollars are funneled into new programs, someone or some group is essentially controlling and influencing the direction of your schools and students' lives. Think, for example, of the parental outrage over sex education programs that promote "safe sex" even among young teenagers.

In 1994, *Education Week* conducted an informal telephone survey "of sources in state legislative education committees and governors' offices to determine which education groups have the most influence in shaping education policy."[1] The following rank order from most to least influential was found:

- Teachers' unions
- Education departments
- School boards
- School administrators
- PTAs

In addition to the influence of these groups on our educational system, Cliff Schimmels, in his book, *Parents' Most-Asked Questions about Kids and Schools*, adds three more:

- Parent groups and special committees
- Textbook publishers
- Individual classroom teachers[2]

Schimmels's reference to the importance of parental involvement, curriculum, and teachers is helpful in understanding all of the forces that come to bear on our schools.

What are the implications of these findings, and what might you be able to do in your community?

Pushing the Right Buttons

Knowing how to put pressure on each of these key groups is essential. Remember those large, federally funded programs mentioned earlier that control the direction of public education? Political persuasion via organizations consistent with your values is very effective at the federal and state levels, particularly when voters call or write their representatives during politically sensitive times. Organizations such as the Christian Coalition, Focus on the Family, Concerned Women of America, and the Family Research Council and their local and state counterparts, Family Policy Councils, wield tremendous influence. Political leaders respond to pressure, and we can "turn up the heat" on issues of importance to us by supporting such organizations.

Teachers' Unions

Teachers' unions are made up of people on the front lines, and if we want to bring about educational reform, we cannot ignore their influence. Even if we disagree, it's important to maintain a healthy rapport with them whenever possible.

Many Christian teachers we interviewed see the need for unions, even though they do not agree with many of the unions' policies. Today there are alternatives for those teachers. Two conservative teachers' organizations are growing rapidly: the Association of American Educators and the Christian Educators Association International. (See the Resources section for further information.) We envision a day when they will be regarded as the organizations of choice for better educators.

It's a big mistake to ignore union leaders. Steve remembers well the day a union representative put him in his place and with good reason. Steve had developed a solid relationship with this union representative. He had respect for Steve's work on a statewide initiative, but said, "This is a very important program that will have a direct and positive effect on both teachers and students in our state. If you had only involved me right from the beginning, I would have supported you, but . . . ." By then it was too late. Unfortunately, not involving him in the early development of a costly program needing legislative support cost Steve the union influence that could have leveraged the vote. Imagine the positive impact a conservative, principled, and powerful teacher's union could have in this country!

The larger percentage of those involved in education are trying to improve schools, especially student achievement. We won't agree on everything, but making an attempt to work together for the good of America's children will be worth it.

State Education Departments

In spite of its image of stuffy bureaucrats and its similarities to "Big Brother," state education departments do perform some very valuable functions. In order to set the best pace for school districts to stay competitive in the race for excellence, they distill input from federal sources, legislators, governors, school boards, professional associations, unions, and other citizen groups to formulate vision, policy, and direction for student learning. Major policy changes, often driven by legislators and teachers' unions, will profoundly affect what happens in your child's classroom.

When parents have no success dealing with their local school boards and school officials over matters of serious concern, they can take legal action locally or appeal to their commissioner of education. That is where the buck stops in most states and can be the place where concerned parents and taxpayers finally get action. Even if your request is denied, the media publicity alone is often enough to make big waves in your school district. At the very least, the commissioner can serve as a safety net for the most serious problems.

One of the easiest ways to keep abreast of what's happening in education is to contact the federal and state education departments' Internet sites on the World Wide Web. These sites will provide valuable information on state policy and new direction in curriculum, instruction, assessment, and many other important developments. This type of information is very helpful as you work to improve the schools in your community. Utilizing the Internet will help you become as informed as your school leaders. (You will find major Internet sites in the Resources section at the end of this book.)

Who's Responsible?

When we talk about who is responsible for the effectiveness and efficiency within individual school districts, boards of education and school superintendents quickly come to mind. It's important to know exactly what they do.

Boards of Education

Boards of education set the tone for schools in their community and should reflect the desires, values, and expectations of the taxpayers. In most states, they are also legally responsible for school districts, for developing and implementing the budget, for the hiring and firing of teachers, principals, and superintendents, and for relating to school and community. Dissension on the board is always reflected in dissension among the ranks of teachers and townspeople alike. A reasonable, well-informed, responsive board is the ideal, but not often the reality.

Electing the Best Candidates

School board elections are a political hotbed in many towns and cities across an increasingly diverse America. It's here at the grassroots level that conservative parents can have their biggest influence in three ways:

1. actively soliciting the candidacy of the most highly qualified people to run for election;

2. helping them get elected through every honorable means, including literature campaigns, public forums, radio talk shows, and effective letters to the editor of the local newspapers; and

3. praying for them once they are elected.

America's school boards are a picture of democracy at work. In a society and culture that values democratic principles, school boards play a vital role in supporting and applying those principles. U.S. Secretary of Education Richard W. Riley said recently:

> We are, my friends, at the door to a new time. And, in this new era, we will not build with bricks and mortar. We will build with minds— with the power of knowledge—and with the talent of every well- educated American who is eager to participate in our free enterprise sys- tem and strengthen our democracy.[3]

When school boards operate democratically, considering parents' views and involving the community in the development and implementation of a shared vision of what their schools could become, then students, and ultimately our nation, will benefit greatly.

Debbie Hitchcock is a parent who stood up for a conservative school board in her community, often without much support. Over the years, through persistent networking, maintaining a courteous and helpful attitude, and well-informed persuasive dialogue, her efforts have begun to be successful. She advises: "A *united effort* by committed Christians could affect school policy by gradually replacing school board members, gaining a board majority, and then bringing about school reform. However, this takes a long-term effort, because most of the seats are won by numbers." Like anything else, networking drives voters to the polls and gradually the tide swings. The place to begin positive school reform must include electing a responsive and largely conservative school board.

Often it seems we have little to say about how our schools are run, but experienced educators like Cliff Schimmels disagree:

> I am just naive and simple enough to believe that private citizens have almost all the say in the way schools are run. In spite of all the talk about federal court decisions, in spite of all the talk about state legislation, in spite of all the talk about the power of educators and administrators, I still believe in the power of the local school board, and in most places that board is composed of private citizens.[4]

We believe Dr. Schimmels. The major control and influence are still yours. Let's take his advice and believe we can influence the system and make a difference in our schools and communities.

Superintendents of Schools

A superintendent has a thankless and endless job. From a leadership perspective, the superintendent's role is pivotal. A superintendent must be knowledgeable in curriculum, instruction, assessment, and staff development in order to be respected as an educational leader in his or her school district.

Equally important, a superintendent has a relational role and sets the tone for the culture of learning as he or she interacts on a daily basis with parents, board members, teachers, staff, and students. Attitudes and values, whether academic or behavioral, trickle down from the top. Modeling desired behaviors has a powerful effect on learners, no matter what age. When superintendents exude enthusiasm for excellence and fairness, everyone within their sphere of influence will be positively motivated to achieve. Good superintendents are worth their weight in gold.

Communities and their children benefit when these superintendents work well with the board of education. School districts can run amuck programmatically and financially when conflict pervades these delicate relationships. A very special mix of vision, influence, motivation, drive, and community support is needed to make schools flourish, and a good superintendent is the magic in the mix. Positive, upbeat, high-integrity leadership combined with clearly stated content and performance standards can provide sound beginnings for school improvement in your community.

Unfortunately, a poor superintendent can ruin morale from the lunchroom to the bus garage and everywhere in between. Recently we heard of a school district where half the faculty wanted to quit because of a badly managed district. It doesn't take long for a miserable faculty to propagate miserable students and equally miserable parents. If your district has this problem, speak with members of the board of education and find out if anything is being done to remedy the problem or replace the superintendent. Your children and the morale in your school are too important for you to remain silent.

Although everyone will not agree, there is a bright side in a growing trend toward accountability and honest reporting of school effectiveness. The golden days when schools simply announced their needs and taxpayers leaped to their aid are gone. Now we want to see how our tax dollars are spent and whether they are building effective learning environments for our children. Accountability isn't a pleasant experience for schools, but we all know pruning produces better fruit in the long run. Keep pruning!

Parent/Teacher Associations

In many communities, PTA meetings are notoriously underattended. When both parents are working outside the home, or when only one parent is present, there hardly seems time for basic maintenance, much less finding time for one more meeting a month. Yet, parents who devote even small segments of their time and attention to what goes on in school, what teachers need, and the current concerns facing their public school will find doors opening and people listening to them when needed.

Textbook Publishers

Textbook issues can polarize schools and conservative parents. Christian parents are raising their voices loud and clear about unacceptable content, particularly of science, health, and social studies texts. In nearly every community strong objections, scathing letters to the editor, and hot debates at board meetings have centered around required reading that compromises Judeo-Christian values. As culpable as schools may be, let's not ignore the textbook publishers. Any public outcry that affects their competence, their standing, or their pocketbooks will cause them to reconsider their market. Consider a letter campaign or petition to communicate your concerns. Seek acceptable alternative choices by contacting organizations such as those listed in the Resources section at the end of this book.

Classroom Teachers

The bad news and the good news are the same: When the classroom door closes, real school reform begins or ends. The bottom line is the individual classroom teacher relating to your son or daughter. It is vital that you know your child's teacher and communicate regularly, positively, and courteously with him or her. Here are a few simple ways to do that:

- Drop by the classroom after school hours at the beginning of the year to introduce yourself and indicate your desire to help your child do well in his class.
- Always look and speak your best. First, second, and third impressions count.
- Communicate concerns as soon as there is a problem through a phone call or request for an appointment.
- Aim for solutions, not confrontations. Begin by saying, "How can I help my child with this?"
- Write notes when thanks or appreciation are due.

It's absolutely critical for us as difference makers in our local school district to understand the infrastructure of decision making and change. But there's an even bigger engine driving the changes in Washington and in your state capitol. In the next chapter we'll see how federal and state controls pull the strings behind every classroom in America.

Chapter Highlights

- Teachers' unions
- Education departments
- School boards
- School administrators
- PTAs
- Parent groups and special committees
- Textbook publishers
- Individual classroom teachers

Key Thought

Programs that get the most money may also be driven by particular philosophies of education that may not be compatible with your community's vision for education or your worldview. When millions of dollars are allocated for new programs, someone or some group is essentially controlling and influencing the direction of your schools and students' lives.

What You Can Do

1. Why not make appointments with the big three educational leaders in your school district: the board president, the superintendent, and the local union president? Each should be able to answer questions such as the following:

   - Is the superintendent or board of education ultimately, even legally, responsible for fund expenditure and use?

   - How do you make sure the schools are accomplishing what the community wants them to accomplish?

   - What are the district's learning standards, curriculum and instructional strategies to reach these standards, assessment, and reporting strategies for monitoring continuous improvement?

   - How was the community engaged in and informed of these activities, and does the community help with strategic planning?

   - Was a picture of the costs and expected benefits presented for each proposed change or strategy?

2. Find out who the union representative is for your school district. Contact him or her and express your concerns. Ask what issues are currently affecting students and teachers.

3. Join your PTA and introduce yourself to its leaders. Learn what's already being done to bring "principled persuasion" to bear on the issues concerning you.

Chapter Eight

The Engine That Drives Change How Federal and State Controls Affect Your School

The goals of public education are too ambitious, and to a degree, they conflict with each other. Public schools have become "warehouses" of children . . . even beyond that, they are becoming more and more a means of social engineering. **Donald T. Carlson, taxpayer and grandparent**

Do not conform any longer to the pattern of this world, but be transformed by the renewing of your mind. Then you will be able to test and approve what God's will is—his good, pleasing and perfect will. **Romans 12:2**

It's been said, "Bureaucrats are the only people in the world who can say absolutely nothing and mean it." Anyone who has waded through layers of bureaucratic nonsense to get a straightforward answer to his question knows exactly what this means. Today, however, bureaucracies mean far more than a ballooning education department. To the conservative, concerned public, they often communicate indifference and a liberal agenda.

Education is a people business. Changing education requires the development of meaningful relationships with many diverse groups of people at the federal, state, and local levels. In order to understand the direction local schools are taking, we need a basic understanding of the federal and state education departments that are driving those changes, including size, cost, and effectiveness. Knowing how to best bring "principled persuasion" to bear on the direction the federal and state leaders take will mean pushing the right buttons until morally defensible change occurs. This is no small task.

How Big Is "Big"?

Like the Empire State Building on the New York City skyline, the public school system in America looms as one of the largest and most complex bureaucratic structures in the country or, for that matter, in the world. Composed of 14,400 districts, 84,705 schools, 2.6 million teachers, and over 44 million students, it touches every individual and family in the nation. Just ask yourself and others you know whether they were educated in a public or private school. Nearly 80 percent of the people you ask will say, "I went to public schools."

How Much Is "Expensive"?

Good schools do not come cheaply. There are significant costs associated with educating over forty million students. Approximately $243 billion are spent on K-12 education throughout the country every year. That's expensive!

Compare that level of spending with the budgets of any large corporation. Even businesses doing one billion dollars a year are considered large and sophisticated. Spending in America for K-12 education actually exceeds by many times the value of multi-billion-dollar industries such as AT&T, Time Warner, and General Electric Corp.

Schools, in contrast, don't make any money. They just consume it, billions upon billions, year after year. It's no wonder politics, passion, and even intrigue pervade the educational policy arena. Unfortunately, it never gets cheaper. Think for a moment: In fifteen years, what will be the cost of a good college education? Most estimates are above $200,000. That's hard to fathom.

Federal spending on pre-K through grade 12 education is expected to increase dramatically by the year 2000. On February 6, 1997, President Clinton sent his 1998 budget to Congress, requesting $29.1 billion in discretionary funds for the U.S. Department of Education. This would mean $2.9 billion (11%) more than in 1997 for "discretionary funds," which include most elementary and secondary programs and some post-secondary programs, but not student loans. Some of the proposed increases would include:

- $605 million for Goals 2000 state grants, a $129 million increase
- $500 million for educational technology, a $243 million increase

- $100 million for charter schools, a $49 million increase
- $360 million for Eisenhower Professional Development state grants, a $50 million increase[1]

Federal spending in New York State increased from $448 million in 1975 to $1.5 billion in 1995, more than tripling in twenty years. New York State itself spent $24.94 billion on K-12 education during the 1994–95 school year, up from $13.24 billion ten years earlier. That's an 88.3 percent increase over a ten-year period.

How do communities find the money to support public schools, especially when businesses leave and lower the tax base? Many senior citizens, finding it impossible to keep up with ballooning local taxes on fixed incomes, have sold their homes and left their secure and familiar neighborhoods. We ought to be deeply concerned when this type of community breakdown occurs.

Two very important questions need to be considered:

- How much money do other states spend on education?
- Are the sharp increases in spending for education justified, and do they indicate a commensurate increase in student achievement?

The chart below ranks representative states by total annual expenditure. These costs are taken from "Public Elementary and Secondary Education Statistics: School Year 1996–1997," produced by the National Center for Education Statistics.

Representative States	Estimated Expenditures*
California	$30.274
New York	$24.532
Texas	$20.944
Pennsylvania	$13.020
New Jersey	$12.441
Florida	$12.020
Michigan	$11.039
Louisiana	$ 3.531
Iowa	$ 2.873
Mississippi	$ 2.099
Maine	$ 1.323
Vermont	$ 0.754

*Estimates, in billions, for K-12 education for 1996–97 school year

The amount of money allocated for education in these states is related to the cost of doing business in these states and the size of the student population. There is a $29 billion difference in spending between California and Vermont, which is not too surprising since there are more cows in Vermont than people! Even so, total annual expenditures may not provide the best picture of funding for education.

The amount of money spent on each student provides a better picture of educational spending. The following chart taken from information provided in the National Center for Educational Statistics report orders these representative states on expenditures per pupil:

Representative States	Estimated Expenditures*
New Jersey	$10,189
New York	$8,684
Pennsylvania	$7,204
Vermont	$7,068
Michigan	$6,642
Maine	$6,052
Iowa	$5,696
Texas	$5,498
California	$5,469
Florida	$5,365
Louisiana	$4,541
Mississippi	$4,163

*Estimated education spending per pupil in 1996–97 school year

Note that the per pupil expenditures vary considerably between states. California spends the most and yet is close to the bottom in per-pupil expenditures. And, there is a $6,026 difference in per-pupil expenditures between New Jersey and Mississippi. There are big differences among states in the amount of money going into buildings, salaries, and transportation. How does your own state compare nationwide? For a complete listing of overall and per-pupil expenditures in all fifty states, see the appendix at the end of this book.

The Money Tree

Although federal and state support for education is considerable, the largest percentage of money for education still comes from local property taxes. In a typical suburban school district, 60 percent of income for schooling comes from local taxes, 35 percent from state aid, and 5 percent from federal tax revenues. Roughly 72 percent of that money goes to salaries and benefits. That's a big slice of the pie. And the pie is getting bigger every year. Is student achievement getting better every year?

Dollars Don't Buy Results

Unfortunately, throughout the country student achievement has lagged behind surges in spending. As reported in "Quality Counts: A Report on the Condition of Public Education in the 50 States," a comprehensive report on school effectiveness issued by *Education Week* in 1997:

> Student test scores have inched up, with some real improvements in math and science. But, overall, student achievement is about the same or only slightly better than it was in the early 1970s. Scores on the National Assessment of Educational Progress—which tests a representative sample of students nationwide—indicate that fewer than half the students tested can do challenging work at their grade level.[2]

It is common knowledge that Scholastic Aptitude Test (SAT) scores have declined dramatically since 1963. David Barton did a comprehensive analysis of this decline and ruled out factors many thought should have explained the decline, such as:

- increases in the number of students taking the exam,
- more students staying in school,
- fewer students taking math courses, and
- an increase in the number of minorities staying in school who are taking the SAT.

Barton also provided evidence that classes actually got smaller and both teachers' salaries and per-student expenditures grew considerably during this same time period.[3] With costs increasing and student achievement decreasing, there is no question that we need to scrutinize spending in our schools. Concern over the cost-effectiveness of our educational system is at an all-time high and with good reason.

In a 1994 article on the effects of increasing spending on schooling, Eric Hanushek stated that nationally "over the past 25 years, real expenditure per pupil has risen more than 100%, while all available evidence suggests that performance has at best remained constant but has more likely declined."[4]

When costs are compared to effectiveness, Catholic schools often make public schools look inept. Even when they are only blocks apart in the same city, some less costly parochial schools graduate better-educated students than their public-school counterparts.

Additionally, parochial schools spend less on education than public schools, and yet a higher percentage of their students actually graduate from college. *Education Week* reported on research by Derek Neal, an economics professor at the University of Chicago, concluding that "Catholic schools help improve the economic future of their urban minority students by seeing that more of the students become college graduates, who tend to earn more than those without a degree."[5]

What can we learn from Catholic schools? The important factors in their success appear to be a moral and committed faculty, family involvement, and community support, even when less money is available.

National Control and Influence

In Washington, national control of education is battled out between the legislature and the president, and at times the Supreme Court, with issues such as school prayer and desegregation. However, there are other individuals and organizations that can also strongly influence education, which is both good and bad.

Unions

The National Education Association (NEA) is one of the most liberal and influential organizations in the country, with an annual budget well over $100 million. The NEA's membership of over two million teachers has a great deal to say about what happens in education across the country. They meet with education leaders and influence policy directly. They push hard to get liberal presidents elected and battle against vouchers and charter schools. When the NEA speaks, government listens.

Universities

Faculty at major universities also shape education policy in Washington. For example, Marshall Smith, a well-known college professor, currently works as deputy secretary of education. Mr. Smith wrote some of the seminal papers on "systemic educational reform," which is the reform model operating throughout the country today.

Individuals

It is common knowledge that the School-to-Work movement in America is heavily influenced by Dr. Marc Tucker, president of the National Center on Education and the Economy. He has been in direct contact with First Lady Hillary Clinton and now serves on the National Skills Standards Board setting learning standards in occupational and career education for students throughout the country. Influencing education policy is often on a person-to-person basis. Never think that the actions of just one person can't change the direction of education at the national level. You could be that person.

Organizations

The government also responds to well-backed and well-supported conservative organizations such as the Family Research Council. Using "principled persuasion," the Family Research Council is a strong advocate in Washington and on national radio for pro-family issues. By providing trustworthy information and analysis, it advises the public how, when, and why to contact congressmen. Exerting influence can be as simple as writing a letter, making a phone call, or writing a check to support the efforts of organizations that are making a difference.

State Control and Influence

At the state level, education policy is set by the legislature and governor, but what goes into each law is heavily influenced by the state education department, school board association, teachers' union, superintendent's organizations, and others.

State Education Departments

State education laws are translated into regulations by most state education departments. These regulations guide what schools can and cannot do and usually focus on the safety and health of children. More recent laws and regulations are defining parental involvement in local decision making and monitoring how well students are achieving the state's learning standards, as well as other measures of school success.

State governments are heavily involved in what local school districts can and cannot do and what they must focus on in order to receive both federal and state tax dollars, which come directly from you, the taxpayer. State education departments manage great sums of money from federal programs such as Goals 2000 and School-to-Work.

State-level Exams

States heavily influence the direction of education when they develop and administer state-level exams that must be passed by all students in the state. These exams exert pressure at the local level by measuring the state's learning standards and are often used to issue diplomas with special levels of honor or performance. It should be noted that neither the governor nor the legislature is involved in test development, making the state education department's impact on the local school district substantial.

Direct Pressure

It is possible to change the direction of education in states by direct pressure. Mrs. Phyllis Schlafly, of The Eagle Forum, helped halt outcome-based education (OBE) in Pennsylvania. State education departments are often intimidated by such organizations as The Eagle Forum, which continues to battle OBE, School-to-Work, and Goals 2000 activities at the state level.

Now that you understand how things work at the local, state, and federal levels, let's look at what's really going on inside the school doors across America.

Chapter Highlights

- How big is "big"?
- How much is "expensive"?
- The money tree
- Dollars don't buy results
- National control and influence
- State control and influence

Key Thought

Schools, in contrast, don't make any money. They just consume it, billions upon billions, year after year. It's no wonder politics, passion, and even intrigue pervade the educational policy arena.

What You Can Do

1. Ask the president of your local board of education for a copy of your school budget. If you are new to the district, ask how well voters have supported the budgets in recent years. If you feel qualified, you might offer to serve on a committee that reviews the school budget each year.

2. Ask school officials what percentage of your local budget is derived from federal moneys and what constraints are placed upon your school in order to receive those moneys.
3. Many states are refusing Goals 2000 money. Write your congressional leaders and suggest your state do the same.

Chapter Nine

Oceans of Reform Surviving the Waves of Change

I'm concerned about the changes that have taken place in our reading curriculum from phonics to whole language, about the changes from time-honored methods to anything new , even if it's experimental. As my youngest child now enters the school system, I need to be more involved than I ever was before. **Linda Abate, parent**

A wise man has great power, and a man of knowledge
increases strength. **Proverbs 24:5**

We were agreed. Spending a week on the Outer Banks of North Carolina was one of the best vacations we had ever had. Nearly twenty members of Steve's large family had pooled their resources to rent the grandest ocean-side home we had ever seen. It was huge! The great room in this place was bigger than the entire first floor of our house! What fun we had enjoying the luxury of being together in such a breathtaking setting.

During one of our many walks on the beach, we noticed a bottle bobbing up and down on the crashing waves. It rolled and bounced from wave to wave, seemingly headed nowhere. When it finally landed on shore, we were disappointed to find there was no message inside! Why would anyone seal a bottle and throw it out in the ocean with no message, no purpose?

How like today's public schools, lurching from one wave of reform to another with no apparent direction. Each surge bounces our schools to and fro, with no clear goal in sight. After a momentary lull, when things begin to quiet down, *boom!* Another powerful reform wave hits, throwing education on yet another uncharted course. How can schools survive? One sure way is by recognizing the waves most likely to hit and keeping our eyes on a more certain shoreline.

If your district is caught in one of the more powerful reform waves of the '90s, such as Goals 2000 or School-to-Work, hold on. It may be a long, exhausting cruise. Sadly, our federal navigators don't appear to have our children's best interests in mind.

Educational reforms may come and go, but they carry a lot of power. Although that seems frightening, they can also be used to great advantage by wise school leaders who know how to envision the future, plan carefully, and integrate funding sources to accomplish local goals. Your job may be to help your schools reach a desirable and safer shoreline.

It seems like a new educational reform is reported in the press every month. The headlines usually read something like, "New School Improvement Model Proposed by Dr. Doolittle at Local University Guarantees Success for All Students!" or "State Education Department Proposes New Strategy Guaranteeing All Students Will Graduate on Time."

The history of educational reform has been dotted with similar declarations since the early 1900s. The call to arms gets especially heated when student achievement stagnates or declines and costs skyrocket, as they have for the past thirty years. Gary Bauer, in his book *Our Hopes Our Dreams*, notes these alarming statistics:

> Only one-third of the nation's high school seniors are proficient readers, down another 10 percent in just two years. Violence is rampant. Sixty percent of urban schools responding to a National School Boards Association survey in 1993 reported student assaults on teachers. Roughly 135,000 guns are brought into schools every day. The United States spends a higher percentage of its gross national product on education than do Germany, Japan, South Korea, France, Great Britain, and other countries, yet it lags behind them all in educational outcomes.[1]

Our schools will have a strong effect on the nature of our society throughout the twenty-first century. Higher student achievement in the core academic subjects must become our top priority. Our schools are simply performing too poorly, particularly in the inner cities, and we must do something about it.

In his article, "School and Family in the Postmodern World," psychologist David Elkind summarized the large-scale changes that have occurred in our society over the last 150 years and noted that our schools "mirror the kinship, structure, sentiments, values, and perceptions of the permeable family."[2] This "permeable" family includes rampant divorce, same-sex "marriage relationships," latch-key kids, and consensual sex. Is it any wonder our equally permeable schools now have compulsory drug and sex education, distribute condoms, and set up health clinics within the schools? What a world to raise kids in!

The conservative public has allowed unacceptable changes in schooling, health, and welfare programs by being too silent too often and relatively uninvolved in the decision-making arena. Too few voices have been raised against these new programs and their high price tags.

Regarding school reform efforts, it's worthwhile noting the striking similarity between conservative thinking and centralized/back-to-basics reform efforts, contrasted with liberal thinking and decentralized/progressive reform models. Keep in mind that someone's worldview is often driving the basic nature of a particular reform and that worldview may differ dramatically from yours.

Let's take a closer look at the major waves of reform currently washing over schools throughout America and discuss some actions you might take to prevent further erosion of the beachhead of learning in our communities. As we conclude this book, you will get a clearer view of our goal: healthy schools that deliver a quality education in a moral climate. But first, we must define what educational reform really means and identify the major waves hitting our beach.

Major Educational Reform Strategies

Major educational reforms are long-lasting changes in the purposes of schooling, how students are taught, and how schools are funded, run, and held accountable.

Systemic Reform

If you are upset with your school, it is probably due to systemic reform. The goal of systemic reform is to reinvent the entire educational system, accompanied by expected changes in society and the workplace that many conservative Christians will find unacceptable. In the simplest terms, systemic reform includes four basic components applied to all levels of our educational system:

- setting intellectually challenging academic and vocational/technical learning standards for all students;
- testing student knowledge, skills, and, if necessary, attitudes and values;
- building school capacity to help students achieve prescribed learning standards; and

- reporting progress in student achievement and other indicators of school effectiveness and efficiency directly to the public.

The power of the systemic reform model should not be underestimated. It is "top down," heavily funded, highly organized, and carefully advocated. When it is applied simultaneously at the federal, state, and local levels, it's like a huge tidal wave that affects everything in its path. It's moving forward whether you understand it and whether you are on board.

Systemic reform is appealing to many because it marshals the huge educational system operating in America today and is a setup for systematic funding of programs such as Goals 2000 that are aimed directly at improving student achievement of high-level learning standards. It works well with institutionalized organizations, such as the Department of Education in Washington and your state education department. Big government is accustomed to setting goals and priorities and throwing large sums of money into strategies to see that these goals are met. School districts have to agree on the regulations governing the use of the funds. Often those regulations conflict with your value system.

This conflict is illustrated in Kentucky and its comprehensive Kentucky Education Reform Act (KERA). The new federal education laws encourage the integration of funding and programs, thereby allowing school districts to provide health services directly to students.

School Health and Social Services

Providing social and health services at the school site is a warning sign of the diversity of programs that can be brought under the umbrella of systemic educational reform. Make sure that your school district has fully explained to your community the scope of any similar provision of social and health services to students and the justification for such programs.

Systemic reform is beginning to coordinate educational, health, and social policy at the federal and state levels. This type of policy development is difficult to challenge because it is so pervasive. It is the type of "welfare-state" policy that can lead to dependency; its intent appears socialistic—big government will solve all of your problems, they just need half your wages to do it.

Based on America's dissatisfaction with public schools, it is very likely that systemic reform efforts will increase throughout the country. What you should be looking for is whether federal and state mandates are completely overriding local beliefs, values, and priorities for educating and caring for your children. If you find out that they are, get involved and begin asking for details and justifications for these new programs.

Systemic reform efforts are powerful, especially when major programs and funding streams are integrated and states are told that local school districts must support the national goals, or no funds will come their way. Some of the most expensive legislation managed by the U.S. Department of Education includes:

- Goals 2000: Educate America Act;
- Improving America's Schools Act (IASA); and
- School-to-Work Opportunities Act.

Each of these acts is systematically related to each other and is designed to build local capacity to achieve the national education goals. Their combined effect can reach every public school in the nation. They are being used by some "social engineers" to restructure elements of our society.

Virtually every Christian pro-family effort in the country is calling for the repeal of these three programs and the dissolution of the Department of Education. It is the biggest tidal wave to hit schools in the past thirty years. What does each program include?

Goals 2000: Educate America Act

What is Goals 2000, and where did it come from? The Goals 2000: Educate America Act was signed into law on March 31, 1994, by President Clinton and was touted as a comprehensive framework for school improvement across the entire country. Goals 2000 is designed to be consistent with the Improving America's Schools Act and the School-to-Work Opportunities Act. Taken together, these very influential programs are backed by huge sums of money and a philosophy akin to outcome-based education and total quality management—making for heated discussion nationwide. (Outcome-based education is discussed in detail in chapter 5, "Crucial Concerns in the Classroom." Total quality management is critiqued in chapter 10, "Streams of Innovation.")

The main "carrot" in Goals 2000 is a grant program to states and school districts willing to adopt improvement plans consistent with the new education laws. This program is competitive, not formula-based for all schools as is the case for the IASA program. These local school improvement plans "must call for setting high standards for curriculum content and student performance, as well as opportunity-to-learn standards or strategies for insuring adequate school services."[3]

Why Christians are Concerned

All schools in America will be affected by Goals 2000. Even though only a small percentage of local school costs are federally aided, those schools directly receiving Goals 2000 grants will have to meet strong requirements, moving the control of educational reform to the federal level and away from the individual state and its communities. That is cause for grave concern. Education is a state issue, and local control of educational programs is essential.

Goals 2000 grant recipients and schools throughout the nation are expected to achieve the national goals of the Clinton administration. However, the goals the Clinton administration believes are necessary to save America's educational system go way, way beyond the K-12 classroom. A summary of the eight goals follows:

By the year 2000—

- all children in America will start school ready to learn;
- the high school graduation rate will increase to at least 90 percent;
- all students will leave grades 4, 8, and 12 having demonstrated competency over challenging core subject matter, including English, mathematics, science, foreign languages, civics and government, economics, arts, history, and geography;
- the nation's teaching force will have access to programs for the continued improvement of their professional skills and the opportunity to acquire the knowledge and skills needed to instruct and prepare all American students for the next century;
- the United States will be first in the world in mathematics and science achievement;
- every adult American will be literate and will possess the knowledge and skills necessary to compete in a global economy and exercise the rights and responsibilities of citizenship;
- every school in the United States will be free of drugs, violence, and the unauthorized presence of firearms and alcohol, and will offer a disciplined environment conducive to learning;
- every school will promote partnerships that will increase parental involvement and participation in promoting the social, emotional, and academic growth of children.[4]

While all of this may sound rational, the impact on our lives and families could be much more than expected. For example, regarding the goal that every child must come to school ready to learn—does this imply government control of preschool health and education? You bet!

Although there are provisions in Goals 2000 for increased parental involvement and flexibility at the state and local level, the long-term impact on our children and society will be decidedly negative, especially in the areas of academic achievement, self-restraint, and respect for authority. James Dobson summarized the most pressing issues contained in these federal directives as follows:

- With passage of Goals 2000, the control of education in the United States moves to the federal level and beyond the grasp of parents.

- Our schools will henceforth be pushed toward a radical philosophy known as outcome-based education (OBE).

- Parents will get no assistance in paying for the school of their choice.

- There is legitimate concern for family privacy within provisions of the new legislation.

- As was predictable, Goals 2000 opened the door to school-based health clinics and the wider distribution of condoms to adolescents.

- Goals 2000 creates costly new levels of bureaucracy, including a National Education Goals Panel, a National Education Standards and Improvement Council, and a National Skills Standards Board.[5]

It is a fair statement that conservatives were surprised by Goals 2000. The same can be said of School-to-Work. These systemic efforts to restructure the entire educational system in America will move our schools away from a strongly academic curriculum to one geared more to careers and work force preparation.

Improving America's Schools Act

The Elementary and Secondary Education Act (ESEA) was established in 1965 as part of President Lyndon Johnson's War on Poverty. For thirty years it has provided federal assistance to schools, communities, and children in need. The Improving America's Schools Act (IASA) reauthorized the major ESEA programs through fiscal year 1999 to the tune of $9.5 billion annually, the largest federal funding source for K-12 schools.

ESEA programs tend to isolate services to students in "pull-out programs." The newer IASA has been designed to work with other funding sources to impact the entire school learning environment to benefit all students. As reported by the U.S. Department of Education, the guiding themes of IASA include:

1. High standards for all children—with the elements of education aligned, so that everything is working together to help all students reach those standards.

2. A focus on teaching and learning.

3. Partnerships among families, communities, and schools that support student achievement to high standards.

4. Flexibility to stimulate local school-based and district initiative, coupled with responsibility for student performance.

5. Resources targeted to areas of greatest needs, in amounts sufficient to make a difference.[6]

There has been little concern from the public over money spent in the ESEA and IASA programs. This could be because it is a program targeted to students from low-income families, as well as the fact that states distribute the money by formula to all deserving schools. You can be certain that considerable IASA moneys come into your district if you are in a rural area or inner city. Ask your board members how much is received and how it is being used. The new guidelines support improvements in the entire instructional program for all children, not just those labeled "in need."

School-to-Work Opportunities Act

According to the federal government, the School-to-Work Opportunities Act (STWOA) of 1994 "is a bold new approach to federal investment, using federal dollars as venture capital to jump-start state and local community efforts to design and build their own school-to-work systems. The STWOA lays out a framework for coordinating and streamlining all federal youth education and training programs."[7]

Sounds pretty innocuous, doesn't it? What isn't apparent from the federal descriptions of STWOA is the very heavy "social engineering" going on behind the scenes.

There are five underlying principles of School-to-Work:

1. Federal support must help transform vocational education into true school-to-work systems serving all youth.

2. Federal support for vocational education must be streamlined and rationalized.

3. States and local communities must have flexibility to design the systems that work best for them.

4. Federal dollars must continue to be targeted to schools with high concentrations of special population students.

5. Recipients of federal funds must be held accountable for results for students.[8]

The STWOA is fully integrated into the funding of all vocational and technical educational programs throughout the country. These vocational and technical funding programs are designed on the European-style work force preparation systems. These programs are driven by the needs of business and industry, not by parents' interests in a broad academic school program. Therefore, the louder the voice of vocational and technical education, the greater its impact on society.

The combined effect of Goals 2000 and School-to-Work is beginning to restructure schooling and other aspects of life in America. Joe Esposito, in his report on STWOA entitled "Tangled Web," expresses this concern in strong language:

> This total restructuring of our American society is unconstitutional, un-American, and anti-Christian. It will destroy our present American system of free enterprise and individual freedom to choose one's life work.[9]

This may not be far from the truth when one considers the power of computers to classify jobs needed by business and industry. By analyzing student knowledge and skills, students can be channeled into certain career patterns for life! We need to keep a watchful eye on our educational system to make sure that it serves the interests of parents and children, not our business leaders.

In addition to the large-scale, systemic reform efforts being advocated at the federal level, there are many less pervasive models being tested throughout the country. School choice is one of the more significant areas being explored to improve our schools. Let's take a closer look at the choices being offered.

School Choice

Americans and choice go together. Choice is healthy. It is directly related to competition, which keeps expenses in check. Imagine going to a car dealer and finding only one available color of the car you wanted or building a new home with only one set of plans to use. Ridiculous, isn't it? It is impossible to make a sound decision about anything without choice. Yet in choosing your child's school there is little choice, if any, in the public arena. But not for long.

Getting the Best out of Public Schools

There are strong, conservative forces that believe choice in education is the most important pro-family issue to date. Competition pushes performance and controls cost. Choice could produce quick improvements in America's schools.

School choice is catching on in America and it takes many different forms. These new choices may better support your values and beliefs. Some of the many faces of choice in education include:

- public school choice
- charter schools
- vouchers
- magnet schools
- home schooling

Public School Choice

This seems like a misnomer, but in actuality, being able to choose a public school for your child has been around for some time.

The most famous school district supporting public school choice is District 4 in New York City. In 1974, this district started a unique elementary school, Central Park East, under the direction of Deborah Meier. What happened in District 4 is best described in her own words:

> Central Park East, along with more than 30 other small schools of choice begun by District 4 during the next 10 years, was and remains an amazing success story. We lived a somewhat lonely existence for a decade, but today both Central Park East schools and the District 4 "way" have been roughly replicated in dozens of New York City school districts and are now part of accepted citywide reform plans. What the schools that have adopted this model share is a way of looking at children that is reminiscent of good kindergarten practice. Or, put another way, they operate according to what we know about how human beings learn, and they are guided by a deep-seated respect for all the parties involved—parents, teachers, and students.[10]

District 4's public school choice program has proven to be effective; "90% of those who enter high school not only receive high school diplomas but go on to college—nearly double the rate for the city as a whole."[11] What made the difference?

The crucial decision made in the District 4 "revolution" of two decades ago was to create a broad and diverse set of new schools, not to reform existing schools.[12]

This is an important point to remember when your school district begins taking a critical look at self-improvement and perhaps even developing new schools of choice. Meier notes that "it's easier to design a new school culture than to change an existing one. And it's the *whole* school culture—not this or that program—that stands in the way of learning."[13]

Few parents know that public school choice is possible. Nevertheless, this option may be far better than some of the other more controversial approaches to school improvement being considered. However, it takes an unbelievable amount of energy for a community to design and develop a new school culture. It can happen, but it requires faith in school leadership and months of discussion and planning until all parties involved agree on a "shared vision" for their new schools.

Charter Schools

This approach to reinventing our schools is considered the most radical public school choice option available to communities. Chartering? Most of us think of chartering a boat for a vacation. What's the connection? Mark Buechler provides a summary of the basic characteristics of this type of school:

> Charter schools are independent, results-oriented, publicly funded schools of choice designed and run by teachers or others under contract with a public sponsor.
> Teachers, parents, social service organizations, or others develop a contract, or charter, to convert an existing school to a charter school or start a new school from scratch.[14]

The most attractive component of charter schools is their exemption from collective bargaining (only in some states), district policies, and most state education laws and regulations within exceptions of health and safety, building, and fire codes. By the fall of 1996, twenty-five states and the District of Columbia had charter school laws, and there were 481 charter schools operating.

Paul Hayford, who has been tracking charter school legislation and research for the New York State Education Department, has summarized the most common reasons people give for starting these schools:

Charter Schools

"The great appeal of charter schools is that they invite innovation while demanding results—the precise opposite of conventional U.S. public schools."[15]

Some are very idealistic. They believe they have a better idea how to do schooling and they would like an opportunity to try out their ideas. Some believe they have a better idea how to educate a certain population of students, for example, those who are at risk of dropping out. Others want an alternative to their public school either because it is an objectively poor-performing school or because they perceive it to be doing a poor job.[16]

Starting and running a charter school is very difficult and should only be undertaken by persons deeply concerned about the quality of their public schools and who also have a strong vision of what their new school can become. If you are that person, you will have more opportunities to exercise this choice option because many more states are considering charter school legislation. Your state legislator would be a good place to start getting additional information on this important school choice option.

A word of caution is needed concerning the charter school reform movement: Knowledgeable, savvy individuals from any persuasion can develop a team and apply for a school charter. In California, several individuals with clear connections to Scientology are planning to do just that. Is your state a charter school state? Check out what types of schools have received charters and how well they are doing. Perhaps you'll become involved in developing one that is more in line with your beliefs and values.

Vouchers

Vouchers provide financial support for a portion of the costs of private schools, and in some states, at public schools of choice. You may live in a state that already has passed legislation authorizing such vouchers.

Is voucher legislation a legitimate school reform model? Perhaps. It does involve funding and it does give parents some measure of choice in schools. Vouchers can force educators to think twice about the quality of learning services they are offering.

Vouchers, therefore, facilitate school choice for parents, but they don't seem to have the same effect on school quality as experienced in District 4, where the entire community was involved in the design of entirely new schools.

By the end of the 1996–97 school year, voucher legislation had been introduced in fourteen states and anticipated in eleven more. As reported in the *American Teacher,* there are many variations in legislation across the country:

- Texas is considering three voucher bills;
- Arizona is proposing "parental choice grants";
- Florida is considering providing "certificates" or "scholarships" for low-income students;
- Florida and Colorado are considering vouchers for home-schooled students; and
- Congress is considering a number of bills to fund vouchers; one $50 million proposal would set up a five-year demonstration program.[17]

The use of vouchers, both publicly and privately funded, is the most hotly debated school reform initiative in America. One attempt to detract from their effectiveness is that the numbers just don't seem to work. When implemented, too many kids are left out, according to Gerald Tirozzi, a former state commissioner of education:

> A simple mathematical exercise will immediately point out that the numbers don't work. A voucher system, regardless of the amount of money provided, can only accommodate a minimal number of public school students. To think of vouchers as a credible solution to the problems of public education is to disregard most of America's students.[18]

Yet, poor families who want to send their children to private or religious schools would surely benefit from vouchers. In fact, it is such a desirable alternative in New York City that 17,000 applications were received for 1,300 scholarships to Catholic schools. The scholarships were financed by a foundation created by Wall Street executives, and the parental response reflects considerable dissatisfaction with the city's public schools.[19] The voucher issue will not go away. You will probably be exposed to it if you are in a major city, where choice is badly needed to provide better education for young people.

Magnet Schools

A magnet school is a specialized school within a district, sometimes a school within a school. The specialty might be the arts or technology or science. Sometimes they offer multiple specialties such as art and music. Federal funds can be used to support these schools and they have, therefore, increased in popularity, most frequently in urban settings where they may help reduce segregation.

Magnet schools increase choice for parents but are usually in such demand that student assignment ends up being done by lottery. A prime benefit of magnet schools is that both teacher and student have chosen to be there. They are generally smaller than traditional schools and therefore provide a classroom climate more conducive to student achievement.

Home Schooling

This educational option is becoming more attractive to many parents, and it is no longer the sole province of the religious right. Growth in home schooling has been phenomenal, from 15,000 home schools in the early 80s to over 350,000 by 1994 and over 1 million in 1997. Generally, parents remove their children from public schools for social, academic, family, or religious reasons. Some schools are unsafe or allow behaviors that interfere greatly with learning or undermine parental values.

Perhaps the most inviting finding from the research on home-schooled children is that almost without exception, they perform better than students in public schools. They score twenty-five to thirty-five percentile points higher than public school students on most standardized tests. That's an impressive advantage!

The greatest disadvantage is that home schooling removes the salting influence of Christian families and their children from the public school. It is certainly not the only spiritually defensible choice parents can make. There should be serious reasons for removing your children from their daily influence on other children as well as your own influence in the community as parents involved in your local school. Keeping your children in public schools can have a maturing and strengthening effect on their faith that may not be found in home schooling. Many students may come to know Christ as their Savior because your children are in public schools!

Focused Reform Models

Many school-reform strategies have been started by individuals, organizations, or companies with special purposes in mind. Usually, these new strategies or models start out in one region of the country and spread, depending on their effectiveness. The desperate nature of schooling in America is reflected in how quickly some of these innovative reforms are adapted. Following is a brief introduction to some of the new and not-so-new (we've seen them before) reform strategies you may be hearing about in the media. This introduction will give you basic information to use as you learn more about your school's strategies for improving student learning.

Comer School Development Program

This approach to school improvement was started over twenty-five years ago by Yale University child psychiatrist James Comer. His approach is collaborative and community-based, and focuses on both the development and education of children. David Squires and Robert Kranyik at the Yale Child Study Center believe that Comer's program succeeds for two major reasons:

1. It supports a change in school culture, and
2. it focuses on children's development—their total development, not just their speech, language, and intellectual capabilities.

Because children attend school for significant portions of their early lives, their social, moral, physical, and psychological development must be central to the school's mission.[20]

The School Development Program operates through three teams: (1) the parents' program, (2) the mental health team, and (3) the school planning and management team. This school-change model is helping children, especially in urban areas such as the Dallas public schools.

The Comer model must be carefully examined regarding the implications of the school as a surrogate home. There are advocates for this model in high places, and you should be sensitive to the implications of the use of this model in your district. Many students do need help with social and health problems, but is the school setting the proper place for the provision of such services, or is it the child's exclusive learning place?

Coalition of Essential Schools

This famous approach to improving our schools is being used in hundreds of schools across the country and has two unexpected characteristics: (1) It is limited to high schools, and (2) it treats each school as unique. It is the brainchild of Theodore Sizer, director of the Annenberg Institute for School Reform and chairman of the Coalition of Essential Schools, Brown University. In an interview with John O'Neil, senior editor of *Educational Leadership*, Sizer explains in his own words:

In order to be good, a school has to reflect its own community. And, therefore, we offer no model. There's nothing that you just "put into place," nothing to "implement." Our research suggests that you're not going to get significant, long-term reform unless you have subtle but powerful support and collaboration among teachers, students, and the families of those students in a particular community.[21]

This approach to educational reform appeals to most parents. It is open-ended, with seemingly no preconceived agendas, and honest. But there really are differences in what the Coalition emphasizes, especially when compared with other approaches such as Hirsch's Core Knowledge Schools (described in following section).

Sizer's model stresses thinking skills; *how* students learn is the main point, not *what* they learn. The curriculum contains few subjects but is taught in-depth with topics dictated by student interest. Standardized tests should not be used to give a complete picture of a student's intellect, and teachers will coach kids, doing many hands-on projects.[22]

Sizer's schools have a progressive nature as compared with Hirsch's back-to-basics model described next.

Core Knowledge Schools

E. D. Hirsch Jr., professor of English at the University of Virginia, the person behind the development of these schools, would be considered a traditionalist; some might label him a restorationist. His conservative and back-to-basics approach is working in over three hundred schools at this time. You will have no difficulty understanding the philosophy of his model, nor the expected outcomes. It's probably like the school you attended growing up.

Philosophically and practically, there are strong differences between the Sizer and Hirsch approaches. Hirsch feels *what* students learn is most important, not *how* they learn. Tests should be objective measures of achievement. The curriculum should be wide-ranging, but only an explicit set of topics should be covered in each grade. Old-fashioned teaching methods such as recitation can be used.[23] This reform model is so traditional that you will definitely know if your district is using it because it requires considerable community support to implement.

Staff Development

Ask parents what they think school improvement means and they will probably answer, "Well, it means my kids will be doing better in their courses." Is this possible without better teachers? Perhaps, but better teachers and higher student achievement are related. In fact, good teaching is usually defined by how well students are doing. But it is also true that good students, with support from home, can learn in poorly taught classes. That's why staff development for teachers is a strong candidate for improving our schools.

The problem with treating staff development as a reform model is that nobody is sure what to teach teachers. Schools are responding to very broadly defined guidelines from state education departments. School personnel must then translate these broad guidelines into provocative classroom learning experiences for students. That's no easy task.

This makes the teacher's role very challenging. They want to be part of the solution but are not given enough guidance and explicit training. Teachers are being asked to continue their teaching tasks while rewriting entire curricula, instructional materials, and tests. In *Education Week*, writer Lynn Olson questioned John A. Nunnery, a research scientist at Johns Hopkins University, about the relationship between reform efforts and teacher training. Mr. Nunnery said:

> Reform strategies that work are curriculum-based, have extensive and ongoing professional development that helps teachers deal with classroom instruction, and have clear goals that are well-matched to school goals.[24]

Until staff development takes on these characteristics, it will not have the impact on reform that is needed. You will be able to find out whether your district's staff development meets Nunnery's standards. If there is a lack of alignment with the school's major instructional goals, then changes are definitely needed. Additional characteristics of a high-quality, professional development program would include:

- clearly stated goals or objectives that are highly related to student learning standards;

- adult-oriented, practical, focused, with lots of "hands-on" activities;

- scheduled after school or at other times that don't interfere with regular classroom duties (most teachers do not want to be away from their students); and

- periodic, lasting over time until the desired skills and approaches are effective and habitual.

Don't assume that teacher training in your district has these characteristics. Check it out for yourself.

There is a broad continuum of educational reform models available to schools today. Your school district officials should be able to articulate their position on this continuum with regard to philosophy or the big picture, such as "back-to-basics" versus "progressive," or "top-down" versus "school-based" management.

Chapter Highlights

Systemic reform:
- Goals 2000: Educate America Act
- Improving America's Schools Act
- School-to-Work Opportunities Act

School choice:
- Public school choice
- Charter schools
- Vouchers
- Magnet schools
- Home schooling

Focused reform models:
- Comer model
- Coalition of Essential Schools
- Core Knowledge Schools
- Staff development

Key Thought

Regarding school reform efforts, it's

worthwhile noting the striking similarity between conservative thinking and centralized/back-to-basics reform efforts, contrasted with liberal thinking and decentralized/progressive reform models. Keep in mind that someone's worldview is often driving the basic nature of a particular reform and that worldview may differ dramatically from yours.

What You Can Do

Encourage like-minded members of your community to do the following:

1. Insist that new federal and state policies will honor, not displace, traditional family values. Pray for policy makers.
2. Call state legislators and state education department staff for up-to-date school finance and state aid information, and then compare these figures with your school's budget. If federal or state governments are giving your district moneys

not accounted for in local budgets, find out why these moneys are not reported in the school district's budget.

3. Ask your local school administrators how they evaluate the effectiveness of their present reform efforts.

Chapter Ten

Streams of Innovation Recognizing the Good, the Bad, and the Ho Hum

The community is vital, I feel, because communities vote on school budgets. Without necessary funding, we are lost. We have lots of community members in our school volunteering all over the place. In turn, they touch kids' lives who don't ever get to see an adult except in an abusive situation, or from lack of time, not seeing a parent at all. **Christyne Kucera, parent volunteer**

For this reason, since the day we heard about you, we have not stopped praying for you and asking God to fill you with the knowledge of his will through all spiritual wisdom and understanding. **Colossians 1:9**

It was a memorable fishing trip. Steve and his seventy-six-year-old dad stood in the Adirondack mountain stream casting for trout between the rocks in the autumn sunlight, father and son completely content, enjoying the rare treat of fishing together. It was almost too good to be true.

"Look out for those slippery rocks, Dad!" Steve shouted as he saw his father step farther into the stream. But his warning was too late. *Splash!* Down went his dad into the rushing water, pole flying. He bounced painfully on the rocks, then quickly leaped to his feet, a picture of fitness still at seventy-six.

"Wow!" his Dad yelled over the roar of the water. "Didn't think the water was that deep here!"

"Are you OK, Dad?"

"Yeah, no problem, but I can't believe such a small stream could wash me under so quickly. Guess I lost my footing." Wet clothes never stopped him from fishing in the past. Steve knew they wouldn't now either. Crisis past, they continued casting. For a little while, that is.

A couple of hours later, Steve met the same fate. Losing his footing on a slippery rock, he crashed hard into the water, but soon jumped up yelling, blood pouring from his left hand. In trying to stop his fall, he had landed on a broken bottle that caught his wedding ring and deeply cut his finger. Now the fishing trip was over.

Trout fishermen are aware of the hazards in small streams. They can be beautiful and refreshing, but streams are enigmas. It's hard to know when they are dangerous. Innovations in education are much like these streams: attractive, exciting, but potentially troublesome. Schools that do not carefully research innovations before they step in with both feet risk crashing or possibly being washed downstream.

What Is an Innovation?

Innovations are "new" strategies, programs, or activities that occur during a particular period of time. Few innovations succeed and become a true part of everyday school life.

There are many innovations and creative solutions to problems in schools ranging from simple to complex, cheap to expensive. Some simple changes are structural (decrease the number of central administration staff), and some process-oriented (increase staff development).

Big dollars are being spent on innovative programs, and many simply cannot be sustained. This chapter will acquaint you with some innovations that are beginning to pass the test of time, and that may be affecting you and your children today or in the near future. Each description is accompanied by suggestions that will help you find out whether these innovations are right for your school district.

In his book, *Innovation and Entrepreneurship*, Peter Drucker describes the transition from ideas to innovations:

- Ideas that become successful innovations represent a solution [to a problem] that is clearly definable, is simple, and includes a complete system for implementation and dissemination.
- Successful innovations start small and try to do one specific thing.
- Knowledge-based innovations are least likely to succeed and can succeed only if *all* the needed knowledge is available.[1]

Nearly every school innovation summarized below will violate one of Drucker's requirements for successful innovations. The list is short because lasting innovations are rare. Here are the ones we consider the good, the bad, and the ho hum:

The Good

Building-Level Shared Decision Making

Shared decision making is defined as the involvement of parents, teachers, principals, and other members of the community in serious planning and development of educational policy and programs for school buildings and, sometimes, entire districts.

Shared decision making at the school building level is definitely innovative. Schools used to be managed completely without any input from parents, with the exception of the small number who attended school board meetings.

The concern over lack of parental and community involvement at the building level reached a fever pitch at the end of the '80s. In some states parental involvement in building-level decision making was so infrequent and dysfunctional that regulations were written forcing the issue. Today these schools must involve representatives from the community in school planning and decision making. They actively solicit community involvement and send their plan for shared decision making into the state education department for review and approval.

Chris Kucera has spent a lot of time as a parent volunteer on her school's Shared Decision Making team. She reported a stroke of inspiration they had when they decided to put the middle school student newspaper, *The Tiger's Paw*, in the local convenient food market. "The feedback was tremendous!" Chris shared. "Senior citizens loved reading it while having coffee. Who actually votes down many school budgets? Seniors! Now they could see what their school was doing, their athletic teams, and which teachers were there."

Is shared decision making necessary? Absolutely. The effectiveness of the business-as-usual approach can be assessed by a simple question: How many people do you know who regularly attended school board meetings in the past and spoke up about issues of deep concern to them? Today, few schools are run without considerable input from the parents and community members. It's an open door for Christian input.

Are there any problems with shared decision making? Absolutely, and here are a few:

- School districts do not like to be told that they must involve the community in their business.

- The shared decision making committees that are not at the building level, but at the district level, have reduced impact on particular buildings.
- When superintendents have tried to appoint committee members, powerful groups like teachers' unions made sure they had representation or even control.
- Often the committees are *pro forma,* just there in name only, having no effect on educational policy or programs.

Parental Involvement

Jordan hopped off the bus and handed the folded orange construction paper note to his mother. She opened it gently and smiled at his grinning self-portrait and third-grade lettering:

Mommy and Daddy,

Please come to my school for Parents' Night
this Friday at 7 PM to meet my teacher, Mrs. Bains.
She'll have cookies.

Love, Jordan

"Will you and Daddy come, Mommy? Mrs. Bains said she wants both our parents to come." Even at eight years old, Jordan knew the answer was always the same.

"I'll be there, sweetheart, but Daddy can't. He's busy. You know he gets nervous about going back there."

Parents have great influence on their children. A parent's love of learning or distaste for school has a direct effect on their children's acceptance or rejection of learning. Sadly, parents who hated school usually raise children who also hate school.

It will be upstream all the way if the child starts school with negative attitudes. Strong relationships need to be encouraged between home and school to give students a strong start on their educational journey.

Parental involvement in school decision making is one way to do that, and it is definitely here to stay. Take advantage of this new respect for parents. School districts are much more open to your input than ever before. Here are some things you can do that should be welcomed by your schools:

- Find out how well building-level shared decision making is operating in your district. If there is none, take the idea to the superintendent and school board for consideration.
- Ask the superintendent for a list of action committees. These could include curriculum development, test development, technology planning, and others. If

you have skills and knowledge in one of these areas, volunteer to help.

- Volunteer to work on the district budget committee. This committee is important. It operates for many months, seeking community input to keep the community's expectations within budget.

Take advantage of the districts' new receptivity and make a difference.

The Bad

Total Quality Management and Team Building

Total Quality Management (TQM) has been fully integrated into American business and industry for about fifteen years. Since 1990, TQM has begun to seep into portions of our vast educational system, first at the federal and state levels; now even local school districts are buying into it. TQM is a comprehensive approach to management that includes:

- establishing standards of performance,
- learning to work in groups or teams,
- using a group-based, problem-solving model,
- using of statistical techniques and data analysis to improve the system of production,
- focusing on continuous improvement, doing things more effectively and efficiently, and
- eventually reaching a state of mind that is compliant and accepting of change that will quickly lead to product improvement.

In education, the focus of TQM is on (1) learning standards, (2) the use of teams to plan and implement change, and (3) monitoring and reporting student achievement as the basis for improvement.

Why Christians Are Concerned

TQM is not being welcomed into the education arena by some conservative Christians. In fact, it is being painted with the mastery learning and OBE brush, both highly suspect at this time. TQM has been implicated in the development of the School-to-Work Opportunities Act passed by Congress and signed into law by President Clinton on May 4, 1994. National planning for the School-to-Work legislation has a long history tied to social engineering initiatives that are decidedly un-American.

The reason School-to-Work is steeped in TQM is due to the heavy pressure business and industry is placing on K-12 education. Our high schools have been graduating such poorly educated students that both colleges and businesses have had to remediate them, which has angered businessmen. TQM is heavily used by corporate America, so it's natural that hiring students graduating with TQM mindsets and skills will save them money. Some of the reasons we should not travel down the TQM/School-to-Work road are:

- Team-building and problem-solving techniques force students into a "consensus," or average way of thinking, mode. The individual doesn't solve the problem; this might hurt someone's self esteem. Heavy psychological pressure is brought to bear on team members who do not agree with the direction the team is taking. Business and industry are looking for students who are used to working in teams and are compliant. Resistance to rapid change or team consensus building is not acceptable in TQM.

- Systems of occupational assessment are being developed that will identify students with certain industry-friendly skills, attitudes, and abilities. Once students are sorted by computer on these industry-friendly characteristics, they will be pigeonholed into specific types of jobs or job titles industry needs. Labeling students this way could seriously limit their employment options in the future. This type of student tracking into occupations has been used in Europe for decades. Japanese businesses work with high school teachers, keeping track of students who meet their employment criteria. America is the wealthiest and most productive nation in the world, and it didn't get that way following the Japanese or Europeans!

- Databases are being created that may contain such detailed information on students' knowledge, abilities, and attitudes that their privacy is in jeopardy.

Concerns are growing about the application of TQM and team building in education, so we encourage you to stay alert for School-to-Work developments in your community.

The ho hum

Technology and Telecommunications

Most parents would welcome the opportunity for their children to be involved in the JASON Project. The JASON Project is a type of distance learning that includes the use of interactive television between a scientist and students thousands of miles away from one another.

Dr. Robert Ballard is a marine biologist who conceived the JASON Project over eight years ago. He uses small submarines to explore underwater plants, animals, and "treasures" of all types, such as sunken ships of historical significance. He has been involved with finding the *Titanic* and other important vessels.

Dr. Ballard was the first scientist to combine the following technologies to connect his research operation directly to students, live, back in their classrooms:

1. a small submarine for underwater exploration,
2. video and telephone connections from the underwater submarine to the classroom, and
3. joy sticks in the classrooms that students can use to steer the submarine while they watch its direction and communicate directly with Dr. Ballard.

When Dr. Ballard goes down under the ocean on a new research and exploration project, he "takes the students with him." This may seem a little strange, but remember that today's students are "vidiots." They think in video images and can actually "transport" themselves underwater with Dr. Ballard and enter his world. When the students are allowed to steer the submarine from their classrooms, they get a sense of actually being there. He has coined the term "tele-presence" to convey the experience students have when he teaches them about his underwater world of marine exploration.

Not every project is like the JASON Project. Today technology-inspired school reform is cropping up all over the country as a panacea for our educational ills. It can greatly enhance learning or be a great waste of time and money and a poor substitute for the disciplines of discovery.

Technology (i.e., everything from pencils and chalkboards to high-speed desktop computers) and telecommunications (i.e., telephone, radio, television, video conferencing, e-mail, etc.) have always been part of education and learning. Even the use of old slate boards and chalk by students during the last century was a type of technology. Let's explore technology applications in the classroom and see if all the excitement is justified.

Some of the more common ways technology and telecommunications are being integrated into schools in every subject from art and music to science and physical education include:

- Enhancing the writing process by speeding up the "write and revise" cycle as well as allowing students unusual ease in integrating graphics, pictures, and videos into what are now called multimedia compositions. This use of technology is highly motivating to students and provides a freedom of expression not found in classrooms before 1990.

- Simplifying information gathering for analysis and reporting purposes. Using computers and telecommunications, students can actually gather data, graphics, pictures, and videos from around the world. Steve has used the Internet to view pictures in the Louvre on this French museum's World Wide Web site. Imagine the increased capability and quality of student reports using this information gathering tool.

- Using database, spreadsheet, and statistical programs, students can expand their analytical skills in nearly all subject areas.

- Communicating and speaking skills of students are being improved through the use of computers connected to overhead projectors. With these computer-based presentation systems, students present and discuss their multimedia compositions with the teacher and the entire class. Compare this with a standard book review previously read by a student.

It is likely that the technology innovations described here will become lasting components of a high-quality education for succeeding generations. Why then is technology placed in the "Ho Hum" section of this chapter on innovations? The primary reasons that innovative uses of technology fail include:

1. Planning for technology integration in the classroom is done poorly.
2. Technology is expensive.
3. Technology is purchased but teachers are not trained in classroom uses.
4. Student achievement doesn't always go up with the use of technology.
5. Culturally important subjects such as art and music are discouraged or even dropped so districts can purchase more computer hardware.
6. Technology becomes obsolete very quickly.
7. Technology often is underutilized.

Technology can result in higher levels of student achievement or it can literally sit on the shelf and become a very expensive sore spot in a school district that didn't know what in the world to do with it.

Hopefully your district is taking full advantage of innovative learning technologies and parents are informed and supportive. Today, graduating students with no knowledge of computers and telecommunications is definitely a disservice. They will need familiarity with such tools to perform well in college and efficiently on the job.

This overview of school innovations is by no means comprehensive, but it will give you sufficient knowledge of the more common ones to take a closer look at what is happening in your schools and get involved.

Chapter Highlights

- What is an innovation?
- The good:
  building-level shared decision making
  parental involvement
- The bad:
  TQM and team building
- The ho hum:
  technology and telecommunications

Key Thought

Innovations in education are much like these streams: attractive, exciting, but potentially troublesome. Schools that do not carefully research innovations before they step in with both feet risk crashing or possibly being washed downstream.

What You Can Do

1. Ask your superintendent or principal what, if any, innovations are being used in your schools. Hopefully, if you haven't heard about them, the district is piloting them—trying them out before fully adopting them. Also ask if there is research proving, or at least documenting, the effectiveness of the innovation in a school district similar to yours. Evidence of effectiveness must be available.

2. Ask your school board president if building-level shared decision making has been implemented in your district. If the answer is no, encourage the board president to initiate this innovation so more members of the community can have a serious part to play in the development of educational programs in particular schools.

3. Find out if your district has planned for the use of computers and telecommunications in your schools. If not, ask for an explanation why such practical tools are not being considered in your district. Make sure a reasoned approach to technology, including staff development, is being pursued so that important subjects such as art and music are not being eliminated due to technology purchases.

4. Talk with your children about how they use technology in the classroom. Even kindergarten students learn to create stories using computers and their own art work to illustrate them. Ask the teacher if you can observe or even volunteer to help with such projects.

Chapter Eleven

No Small Heroes A Celebration of Christian Educators

I've had chances to go elsewhere, even to go on and finish my Ph.D. I stayed in teaching instead. It drove me crazy thinking about the kids I'd miss teaching.
Jerry Hill, high school math teacher

Love must be sincere. Hate what is evil; cling to what is good.
Be devoted to one another in brotherly love. Honor one another
above yourselves. **Romans 12:9–10**

When we first asked Laura Johnson, a middle school
science teacher, for an interview for this chapter, we explained our purpose was
to honor as heroes those Christian educators who have chosen to remain on the
front lines, to live out their faith as salt and light in the public schools. She
paused a moment, then burst into tears.

"No one has ever said that to me before," Laura sobbed. "Nobody out in
the public has a clue what we do. No one but the kids thanks me, much less
calls me a hero. Thank you so much for saying that to me. It means so much."

How is it possible that those who give so much could be so grossly ignored?
Why do Christian people treat as second best a career spent teaching America's
children in public schools? Is it somehow less spiritual than teaching in Christian schools? Not if we use Jesus as an example. Were he in the flesh today, he'd
be found somewhere mixing with kids. C. S. Lewis once said, "There's no use
trying to be more spiritual than God."[1]

There are many unsung heroes in this country today who exemplify all that
is great about America. Many of them enter a classroom every day and shape

our future. Others provide leadership and support in various forms. They are the dedicated Christian teachers and administrators who are there for the love of kids and the calling of God. We owe them a great debt of gratitude for building excellence and honor into our nation's children. They have remained on a troubled ship and have not given up. In fact, they are among the most upbeat and approachable individuals you'll ever meet.

During the process of interviewing many parents for this book, one question often brought a troubling response. The question was, "Do you know any exemplary Christian teachers or administrators who are making a difference in your school?" Sadly, a number did not. May this chapter open a window for them on some of America's better classrooms. Listen and take a look around. It will introduce you to some of the difference makers we have met and give them the applause and appreciation they so deserve. There are many, many more, and hardly the time and space to do them justice.

◆ ◆ ◆ ◆ ◆

Laura Johnson has been teaching school since 1973, with the exception of taking time off to begin her own family of four children. You may not see her on many committees at church. Laura sees teaching as her ministry. Her face lights up as she talks about the rowdy bunch of middle schoolers she teaches each day.

"Right in the beginning of the school year I point to my front board where I have a sign that says, 'All you need is *agape*' (that raises some questions!) and another with a big heart with the word 'unconditional' on it. I tell them that I love them and that I only have one rule in the classroom: 'Be Cool, Be Kind.' By the end of the year they believe me." In spite of the warm fuzzies these love messages generate, Laura has a reputation for being a strict teacher with high standards. She cannot be manipulated by her students and never plays favorites. Her love for her students gives her an unusual sensitivity to their needs.

"To any teacher I would say, if every day you ask God to use you, you will stumble over opportunities." Laura had just stumbled over one a few days previous to our interview.

"I drove to school one morning and consciously asked God to use me that day. I have about fifty minutes of prep time during lunch, so I went to my car in the parking lot to eat a quiet lunch. For some reason I decided to come back into school before I needed to. I walked down the empty hallway and turned into the student bathroom across the hall from my room. I found a girl whom I didn't know crying hysterically. 'Are you OK?' I quickly asked, feeling a little awkward.

"She nodded and I turned to leave, but I felt the need to turn back and ask, 'Are you sure you don't want to talk to me about this?' I reached out to offer her a hug.

"She smiled and hugged me back, and explained she had just been yelled at by a teacher and had been under a tremendous amount of stress from problems at home. I invited her into my empty classroom where we sat down to talk.

"The first thing I normally ask in an unofficial counseling session is: 'I want to ask you a personal question. Do you go to church?' Based on that response, I know what direction to take. I told her, 'God loves you and cares about you and is waiting for you to ask him for help.'

"Handing her my home phone number, I reminded her that she's never alone and now she also had me. I've seen her several times since, and she smiles and tells me things are getting better. I reminded her that it was no accident that I came in early and found her in the bathroom. God had arranged that."

As a science teacher, Laura deals with controversial issues in a factual way. "A complete education," she says, "is one of the tools for making good decisions. No Christian should fear truth in education." Dealing with evolution is one example. Laura makes it clear evolution is only a theory. She lets her students know creation is also a theory, but they will have to search for the truth themselves. "If evolution were true," she tells her students, "then you would be about as valuable as the chair you're sitting in. The theory you choose to believe affects your whole life."

Regarding premarital sex, Laura lets her students know she believes in 100 percent abstinence before marriage. Once an A student whose parents were both in the medical profession commented: "You actually *believe* premarital sex is wrong? I didn't think anyone believed that any more!"

At the end of every year Laura brings in a one-gallon jar containing a monkey fetus in formaldehyde. It looks shockingly human. "I show them the fetus and tell them that many babies are killed at that size or bigger and it's legal. That's a very strong visual imprint. A baby will never be just fetal tissue to them again."

When asked why she does what she does, Laura answered without hesitation: "It's my calling. When you start with seeing a need and that brings about compassion and that leads to empathy, who can resist being drawn to you? In the process, kids become teachable. That's how you demonstrate your love.

"When you make this bond with kids," Laura adds, "this bond is forever. I have students come back to visit me all the time. The first thing we do is hug. They know I will always still love them." Her students see that love in many ways. We saw it in her tears.

Getting the Best out of Public Schools

◆ ◆ ◆ ◆ ◆

Jerry Hill is a veteran math teacher. He's a fast-paced smile under a pile of slightly graying auburn hair. You can tell he's a runner. Strong and wiry, Jerry strides through the halls with enthusiasm, a ready greeting, and an eagle eye. Kids clean up their act when Mr. Hill goes by. Everybody knows he doesn't put up with bad language or messing around of any kind in the halls. He has a high standard, not only for math but also for life, and the kids love him.

Affectionately referred to as "Hotdogger," he is a clear favorite among his students and respected by fellow teachers as well. When Jerry was recently honored as 1996–97 "Teacher of the Year," they wrote that Jerry "is a mentor and source of inspiration for his colleagues. He sets an example. . . . We all benefit. . . . (He is) the teacher I strive to be."[2]

His students say he's inspired them to do their best. Over 50 percent of his high school seniors are now taking four years of math, which is pretty impressive. Among his graduates are "two who teach college physics (one at Stanford), a Fulbright Scholar, a research doctor at Duke, computer engineers (one of which did a laser eye surgery program), not to mention at least two federal judges!"[3] Jerry is a committed Christian who makes teaching in a public school look easy. How does he do it?

"You have to stand firm," he explained. "You establish yourself because they know you know what you're doing. It's hard for a Christian. If a Christian has the respect of the community, he can express his values, but you have to be careful."

Jerry is clear about his faith and values, but never pushy. In a quiet way, he makes his point. On his wall are hung several interesting posters with biblical quotes, including one painted as a gift for him by a Japanese student with Isaiah 40:31 in both English and Japanese. When faculty committees meet in his room, other teachers often take time to read them. Another poster reads, "What you are is God's gift to you; What you make of yourself is your gift to God." Once, a senior male student asked permission to use that quote in the yearbook. Ten years later that student, now a lawyer and a family man, still visits the Hills.

There have been times, however, when conversations with students led to very direct discussions about Jerry's personal faith. One of his calculus students came right out and asked him one day what it meant to be born again. Jerry answered her clearly, "It means that you affirm your belief that Jesus is Christ, that he is God and that he died for your sins." Seven years later, that student still keeps in touch with the Hills and has attended a Billy Graham rally. "I'm not a pusher," says Jerry, "but I'm not going to hide or skirt anything. You've got to be comfortable in what you're doing."

Like other teachers, Jerry faces a strong current against traditional Judeo-Christian values in today's schools, although he admits his school is much better than some. Recently, a speaker came to Maple Hill High School with a poorly prepared message on the dangers of alcohol and drug use on prom night. His use of foul language and inappropriate stories upset and offended Jerry and many of his students. When the speaker made his closing statement that he was also HIV positive, the kids were so turned off by that time it had little impact on them. Several students met later in Jerry's room to talk with him about the presentation. He went directly to the principal with his concerns. Even though the principal didn't agree with their opinion of the speaker, the point was still made and was received. Perhaps it will have an effect next time someone is invited to give a similar presentation.

Jerry doesn't try to be a buddy to his students, more a father or older-brother figure. "I try to maintain a level of tough love. I love my kids and I'm fair to them, very above board. I don't try to hide their grades or anything from them. You have to be honest with kids so they can believe you have their best interests at heart. They just have to be nurtured and talked to. You have to be available to talk to kids. That's the part about teaching that's so rewarding."

His love for teaching doesn't go unnoticed. When Jerry was nominated for "Outstanding Scholar" at Maple Hill for the third time in four years, Kevin Warrender, the valedictorian, said of him: "Besides math, he also teaches about life. He told all of us about a math mountain we all have. Some of us will continue to climb, others will peak. Because of Mr. Hill, I intend to climb for a long time. The man is a true teacher."

Is that enough to keep Jerry Hill going for awhile? You bet! He adds a personal word of encouragement to fellow teachers: "I wouldn't discourage anybody from going into teaching. The money is a minor issue. We need more Christian teachers in public school. You've got to believe you make a difference. I *know* I make a difference. I'm never discouraged."

◆◆◆◆◆

Step for a moment into the dean's office at a large high school in a sprawling suburban area. That poster hung oddly by the door covers up a hole the janitor will soon repair for the third time this year, where a student put his fist through the wall on the way out.

The dean's office handles the toughest types of problems that a school faces with students. Beyond truancy and academic problems, there are thousands of referrals each year for discipline problems in class, school violence, drug and alcohol abuse, family problems, legal matters, referrals to family court, sexual abuse, and the list goes on.

Meet Dawn Graham, the assistant principal who handles at least half of these problems. What is a lovely, soft-spoken Christian woman doing in a place like this? A lot. Just follow her around for a day, or better yet, step into her private office and listen to her heart. She has a lot to say and has earned the right to say it.

"It's obvious because I work in a public school that I don't think public schools are evil. But many times I am concerned that parents, and I include Christian parents, are not very involved, and I'm not sure why. They don't appear to go out of their way to find out what goes on. The lack of parent involvement has allowed the public schools to take away a lot of the duties and responsibilities as far as education from the parents. They feel powerless."

She has lots of suggestions about ways to correct that. "The elementary school grades are always looking for volunteers. Even if it's only one day a month, be aware of what goes on in the classroom, who the teachers are, and how the school is run. In high school and junior high, every parent should contact every one of his child's teachers. Most parents won't do that, but teachers will respond better to those parents they know are interested. Teachers are overstressed because so many things are expected of them. They will tend to give the best service and the best follow up if they know they will get parental support. If they don't believe they're supported, they are more quick to give up on a child."

How can parents best handle controversial issues? Dawn answered: "A number of parents are aware that I'm a Christian and have come to me with their concerns. It is my experience that if you get some kind of organized group together and if you have a substantive case, not based on your feelings or necessarily something from the Bible, but if there is a substantive case there, and you get together and you persist, you will be heard. There are many groups in a community where people band together and they get their agenda item passed or their philosophy integrated into the school. I think Christian parents have a sense of hopelessness. But I have seen that persistent, prepared parents can make a difference. I'd like to see Christians be more bold."

That's easier said than done. There has been so much criticism of the so-called "Christian Right" that a lot of parents are afraid of looking like kooks. Dawn has some direct advice.

"I don't think they're going to get anywhere if they start quoting Scripture to the school board. If they start saying that something is happening that is against their religious beliefs, a school is not by law required to respond to that. One example is related to our school mascot. Because there are paintings of blue devils on some of the school walls that the kids painted as a school project, one parent investigated and found out that the church of Satan is a recognized church now. Parents are trying to get the school mascot changed as this interferes with the boundary of the separation of church and state."

When we mentioned controversial curriculums, we obviously pushed a hot button. Dawn responded emphatically: "My feeling is that if parents and community were involved before these proposals were passed, like the HIV curriculum, condom distribution, sex and drug education, there is much more likelihood that in its inception stage it would be stopped rather than finding out after it's been adopted by the board of education and is ready for implementation. By then it's too far gone and it's very, very difficult to stop, like a snowball rolling down a hill. Let's get it when it's still small before things get going.

"I see a lot of Christians abandoning the public school system. The cost is very great because we're talking about our young people. I don't see a high level of commitment among Christian or non-Christian families. I see them being too busy with other stuff in their lives."

Regarding alternative parental choices for educating their children, such as private schools or home schooling, Dawn hesitated before answering: "It can be a very positive thing, but if all the Christians were to exit the public schools, what would we have left? It scares me to think what would happen. Although I think home schooling and Christian schools are wonderful, I don't feel comfortable abandoning a system. Not every parent is able to do home schooling and not every parent can afford a private education. Families would be stuck in a system that is more polluted because of the lack of Christian families there."

And yet it's the system, along with its weighty federal guidelines like Goals 2000, that make her job more difficult. "It's a big-brother thing already. There's so much control. But as long as its already there, I'd love to see standards. There's a concern among educators that skill levels are declining and young people are walking out with diplomas but they can't communicate well. I don't think it's a bad thing that we would have federal standards. We need Christians involved at every level.

"I am astounded at schools that implement programs without documented research as to the effectiveness of the programs. It is absolutely insane that children should be used as an experiment. I don't think that we should use the trial-and-error method with our children."

Getting the Best out of Public Schools

By this time, bells were ringing outside Dawn's office, and people were lining up in the outer office with their problems. We didn't have much time left for final thoughts, but she made time to express her biggest concern: the family.

No doubt there is a strong relationship between the deterioration of the American school and the deterioration of the family. Dawn feels parents need to reevaluate their lifestyle. "You really can't be selfish and be a good parent. Parenting is a marathon, incredibly difficult, an exhausting ongoing battle, and yet I do believe that parents are far more equipped to run that race than adolescents. As parents it's our responsibility to set the standard and make the corrections when necessary. I'd like to see parents make a stronger commitment to their children. They may have to give up a second job, or some time working out at the gym or socializing. The cost is that the children will be lost if we don't do that. As loving and caring as parents can be, if that is not demonstrated in loving and disciplining and spending time with your children, it's not going to work."

School reform, in the final analysis, continues pointing at the bigger need, family reform. That's going to take a lot of salt in our society and in our homes.

Would it give you a good feeling as a parent to know that if your son or daughter or student were sent to the school office, there would be someone like Dawn Graham waiting? How many men and women like her do you think there are in the dean's offices around America? We'd like to see many more.

◆ ◆ ◆ ◆ ◆

Next, step in the nurse's office at Charlestown High School in Boston, Massachusetts, and meet school nurse Esther Splaine. She's been described by Matt Daniels, director of the Massachusetts Family Institute, as a "one-woman army, operating within the Massachusetts public schools."[4] Esther has only been at this inner-city high school a year, having come at the invitation of the principal after many years working in elementary schools. And she's been busy. This excerpt from a recent article entitled "Home Court Advantage" by Roy Maynard in *World* magazine gives you an idea what one woman who loves God and kids can do.

> More than 200 ninth-graders filled the auditorium of Charlestown High School in inner-city Boston to hear another presentation on sex. The students were overwhelmingly black and Hispanic, the teachers and administrators almost uniformly white. It looked like an episode of ABC television's *Dangerous Minds,* but with acne.

If any teachers harbored thoughts of ditching the assembly and hiding in the teachers' lounge, school nurse Esther Splaine quickly reeducated them. Their presence was required, too.

On the stage were two doctors from the Massachusetts Physicians Resource Council, part of the Massachusetts Family Institute—one of the leaders in a growing group of state-level family policy councils.

Dimming the lights didn't help much, though. The ineffective shushing of the principals and teachers was drowned out by raucous students, already responding with Beavis and Butthead giggles to the prospect of seeing more condoms on cucumbers.

Mrs. Splaine, a compact black woman and one of the few staff or faculty members at CHS who lives in the Charlestown section of greater Boston, went to the microphone. She was the one who brought in this group of nervous doctors, and she was determined that they be heard. They were bringing something more than the usual safe-sex message, a message Mrs. Splaine sees as sloppy social policy and an arrogant dismissal of her students' potential.

When Mrs. Splaine learned in church of the Massachusetts Physicians Resource Council and its clear presentation of the medical consequences of sex before marriage and the falsity of "safe sex," she was heartened; these willing doctors could fill a void in the lives and education of CHS students.

Without anger, but without much misguided patience, either, Mrs. Splaine brought order to the room. "You sit down and pay attention," she said into the microphone. "These people have something to tell you. And it's something you're not going to hear anywhere else."

The auditorium grew quiet. The students were ready to listen.

One girl in particular, a pretty black girl with cornrow braids on the second row, was becoming agitated. She wasn't hearing what she had expected to hear. Steve Jamison presented the cold medical facts about sexually transmitted diseases and other consequences of premature sexual activity.

Unable to hold back during the question-and-answer session, the girl stood and said to Dr. Jamison, "You've told us all about what doesn't work to protect us from all things. What I wanna know is why haven't you told us what will protect us during sex?" The doctor responded, "There isn't anything. If there was, I would tell you."

Esther Splaine rose from her seat in the front row, walked onto the stage, and took the microphone from Dr. Jamison. "He's telling you the truth, honey," she told the girl. "Remember a couple of years ago, people came in here and talked about 'safe sex'? And then, the next year they came in, they talked about 'safer sex'? Did you ever wonder about why they changed it? It's because 'safe sex' is a lie."

Nurse Splaine told the story of a girl she'd seen in her office that week, who was pregnant but swore she and her boyfriend had used a condom: "There's no way to protect yourself, and that's why I've brought these people in."

In the days after the doctors' presentations, five girls walked into Esther Splain's office, declaring their intention to stop having sex. A Spanish-speaking teacher has asked the nurse if she might translate that presentation, so her Hispanic students could better understand it.

Mr. Daniels' wife, Pat [also a physician], is now working with Mrs. Splaine to start an abstinence support club. And last week, Mrs. Splaine faxed a letter to Mr. Daniels, signed by the school's principal, a white liberal woman who had been dubious about the no-safe-sex message, recommending the program for other public schools.[5]

Wouldn't you love to have Esther Splaine, or her twin, on your school staff? Finding an opportunity to talk with this gutsy school nurse was a challenge. She is *on the move* and readily available to her students. Finally reaching her in her office early one morning, we found her warm, understanding, and a passionate advocate of the kids she serves. And she had a lot to say:

"I called the Daniels because I heard them speak at my church. I invited them to come here. In my building there are nineteen girls who are pregnant. In almost every public high school in Boston there are at least thirteen to twenty-four girls who are pregnant. Every high school has a teen health center, really a teen sexuality center." Part of the problem, she explains, is that the middle class is no longer in the public schools. "Many African-American, Hispanic, and Asian-American middle-class kids are in parochial schools or special 'exam' schools like private public schools, where the work load and standards are higher. Those who don't want to go there apply to an agency called Metco that screens kids and buses them to the suburbs. The public schools have been drained of the cream of the crop. That's why there's an attitude that the public schools have the lower class. But give them the same standards that the middle class has, they will rise to it." Then she adds sadly, "Many of their parents we never see."

At the close of the assembly, Esther related: "The auditorium was silent. The kids asked a lot of questions and gave the doctors a standing ovation. I knew that if teens heard the truth, they'd be better equipped to make decisions. My abstinence group got started within a day or two after the program. By the end of the week I had six, now we're up to seventeen. Sometimes I think they come for the popcorn, cookies, and juice, but they come and talk. They call themselves 'G.A.P.S.: Girls Against Premarital Sex.'"

Now the girls are bringing their boyfriends to meet Esther. She tells them honestly: "Sex is not a tool to be used to keep people. I have five kids. Truthfully, only one was planned. Most of America was not planned! Babies are a gift from God. The only time you can enjoy the gift of sex and babies is when you are married. But when you aren't married and you have sex, it is now two separate families involved and it becomes a problem."

When we asked Esther how the rest of the faculty has responded to her efforts, she said, "I have a lot of support from staff, and many people are excited and happy, but I also believe many people think this is going to fail because it's new and has never happened before."

Recently Esther Splaine has been asked to serve on the Governor's Commission for the Status of Women in Massachusetts. "I want to focus on change and giving information out while I have access to change. I want people to know they have power. We tend to think why it's not going to work. My attitude has been, we serve a God who is so powerful. He's on your team!"

◆◆◆◆◆

Fifth grade might be the last year in school when kids are still kids. Fifth graders still fall in love with their teacher, still love hugs, still believe what adults say. Teaching them is a great trust. Debbie McCoy is a fifth-grade teacher who has been living up to that trust for fifteen years and loving it. She believes in keeping herself accountable to parents.

"At Curriculum Night in September, I tell my parents that I am here to serve them. They pay my salary! I think the school has lost touch with *its* role. If my parents are unhappy, we need to communicate." She urges direct contact between parent and teacher whenever there's a problem and going through the proper channels within the school system. If not satisfied, then go higher up. The greater problem, as Debbie sees it, is busy or absent parents being negligent to prepare their children for the challenges and judgments school requires. "How sad," she says, "that a child could be involved in the preschool program, the breakfast program, the free-lunch program, and the after-school day care program. Today I teach lessons I never dreamed of teaching: lessons on AIDS, child abuse, and adolescence."

How can Christian parents best prepare their children for a public school experience? Debbie advises parents to "equip their children to be both ambassadors and soldiers in the classroom. They should be trained and encouraged to look for opportunities to express Christian principles. If the school day is talked about, situations that required judgment could be evaluated and methods of handling those situations could be discussed."

Are Christians getting "soft"? Debbie has a deep concern that there is a growing lack of discernment in the Christian community. "We cannot be conformed to this world, as Romans 12:2 reminds us, and allow deception to creep in. The minds of our children are a battlefield for the enemy." Challenges to faith are a good cure for softness.

So many Christian parents fear the effect of a secular environment on their children's faith. Debbie sees it as a way for kids to grow more faith. "Parents should remind and encourage their children to get in the habit of praying silently. God will bless them with answers to their prayers and their faith will increase." She's right. Precious to our memories are those times when our own four children found God went to school with them, helped them through difficulties of every sort, taught them about loving others, about forgiveness, and even gave them boldness when a door opened to witness to teachers and fellow students. As their parents, we felt the responsibility to pray them through their school day and celebrated the countless ways God answered. He loves to encourage children's faith and their parents' faith as well.

Debbie loves her job, but like many Christian teachers, it isn't getting any easier. It's often like peddling uphill just to get changes made that will foster a more stable learning environment. For example, she and her colleagues fought hard for a self-contained classroom and won. We feel very much in agreement with her statement that "right now we are at a pivotal point in the history of public education. Key changes will soon be initiated, and with those changes will come confusion as educators try to grab hold of new philosophies, teaching styles, and programs. I agree with many of these changes, but I feel an urgent need to stay well informed, involved, and supportive. I feel that the body of Christ needs to be represented in the educational arena. We need to be viewed as a caring, supportive body who is concerned about the welfare of the whole school. We need to communicate [God's] truth . . . in a way that is not offensive or polarizing."

Debbie McCoy is a realist, not a dreamer. Even when some days seem longer than others, she loves teaching fifth-grade kids, and they know it. And she's committed for the long haul and says so in no uncertain terms: "In no way do I feel like throwing in the towel! God has a purpose and a plan for my life, and each day he equips me with all that I need to be an effective parent and teacher. As long as he knows that I have a sincere desire to walk in his Spirit and in the truth, he will use me no matter what direction school reform takes. I am committed to a life of obedience and accountability to God."

◆◆◆◆◆

Almost everyone has enjoyed the bumper sticker that says, "If you can read this, thank a teacher." Beyond teaching us to read, America owes a great debt to Christian educators in public school like Debbie McCoy, Laura Johnson, Jerry Hill, Esther Splaine, Dawn Graham, and many others. They are teaching us how to live at the same time. We owe them our support through prayer and every form of active involvement. It's time for the millions of spectators to cheer a lot louder for those on the field and think about getting down there and helping them themselves. William Bennett echoes the same sentiment:

> Whatever the reason, until the education world recognizes that real achievement against the odds is a fact evident daily in schools across this country, and that this success depends on committed and talented individuals working hard, then these shining exceptions will remain exactly that—exceptions. There is no federal program, no magic bullet, no novel approach or procedure that will some day be invented to cure the education ills of poor children. It will be done as it has always been done; good schools, good teachers, good principals, and hard work.[6]

We couldn't agree more. How about you? These verses from Philippians 2 are an appropriate encouragement with which to end this chapter:

If you have any encouragement from being united with Christ, if any comfort from his love, if any fellowship with the Spirit, if any tenderness and compassion, then make my joy complete by being like-minded, having the same love, being one in spirit and purpose. Do nothing out of selfish ambition or vain conceit, but in humility consider others better than yourselves. Each of you should look not only to your own interests, but also to the interests of others. Your attitude should be the same as that of Christ Jesus . . . for it is God who works in you to will and to act according to his good purpose. Do everything without complaining or arguing, so that you may become blameless and pure, children of God without fault in a crooked and depraved generation, in which you shine like stars in the universe as you hold out the word of life (Phil. 2:1–5, 13–16a).

Chapter Highlights

- Laura Johnson, middle school science teacher
- Jerry Hill, high school math teacher
- Dawn Graham, high school assistant principal
- Esther Splaine, inner-city high school nurse
- Debbie McCoy, fifth-grade teacher

Key Thought

There are many unsung heroes in this country today who exemplify all that is great about America. Many of them enter a classroom every day and shape our future. Others provide leadership and support in various forms. They are the dedicated Christian teachers and administrators who are there for the love of kids and the calling of God. We owe them a great debt of gratitude for building excellence and honor into our nation's children.

What You Can Do

1. Do you know a Christian teacher in your local public school? Write a thank-you note. It's guaranteed to make his or her day, if not the whole year.
2. Consider how God might have you respond to this chapter, to the words and examples of the teachers you've met here, and to the closing verses from Philippians 2. Write it down.

3. Talk with your children about teachers whom you know to be Christian. Pray for those teachers, for their wisdom, strength, and encouragement. Let them know you are praying.

Chapter Twelve

Tomorrow's Leaders Today Christian Kids in the Public School

It was amazing to me to get together with other Christian kids and just pray from our heart for one another and for our school. Afterwards, kids talked about starting a Bible club on campus and getting together regularly. We talked about how we can witness to our friends so they will see something different in us and that God is really real and that he loves them. We prayed for God to give us a boldness to share our faith with our friends instead of just sitting there. **Angela, high school junior**

In the same way, let your light shine before men, that they may see your good deeds and praise your Father in heaven. **Matthew 5:16**

Five-year-old Jake Smith sat cross-legged on the floor with his kindergarten classmates for their first circle time. "Now let's see who's here!" his teacher began, with a broad smile.

Around the circle, one by one the children shared their names and something special about themselves. "That's wonderful! Now is there anyone else here who we missed?" she added. Jake raised his hand. "Yes, Jake, who did we miss?"

"God!" Jake trumpeted. "God's here!" And his teacher smiled and gave him a knowing wink. No doubt, there was a lot of cheering going on in heaven for this small ambassador.

Those who feel deeply discouraged about America's public schools can rest assured; God has never left. He has his ambassadors everywhere, and they are worthy of respect and applause, particularly those who are students. This chapter is dedicated to these young Christians in public school. We want to honor them and also express our deep appreciation to those who have mentored, prayed for, and in every way encouraged them on their journey.

Recently, early on a September morning all across America and around the world, thousands of Christian middle school and high school students gathered for prayer around the flag poles of their schools at an event called "See You at the Pole." It began as someone's inspiration in 1990 and spread like a fire burning to schools around the world.

Although parents and faculty members were welcome to join them, this annual event is primarily student-sponsored and student-led. Teens arrived quietly, purposefully, reverently, and stood circling their flag. Some held hands or knelt, others stood quietly alone, and they all prayed. They prayed for their school administrators and teachers, fellow students, their nation's leaders, and for one another in a bold public statement of faith. Recently, a local Youth for Christ worker, Dave Lenehan, interviewed many of these kids on Christian radio station WDCD in Albany, New York. Here's what they said about the experience:

"It's great! I think it's really good that kids these days aren't afraid to let people know that, yeah, they love the Lord, and say, 'I'm a Christian,' and they can just come out here and do this."

"I was overwhelmed by how many people are able to come out and praise the Lord with everyone else. It's amazing. It's such an awesome feeling and power that we have together."

"Now there are more people I can talk to, and it'll probably form some new friendships."

"Last year our school experienced a lot of horrible tragedies and accidents in which some students died and some teachers died, and that was very hard. I think it gave a lot of students a loss of hope and a need to search for something more in life. We prayed God would give all of us students hope and a good outlook for the year."

"It was cool. There were about twenty-two people there. Next year we want to double the number. I had a lot of questions beforehand because we had a lot of 'See You at the Pole' bracelets and posters. We have a prayer meeting one morning every week and a breakfast outreach meeting every week where we have some kind of discussion. It was great to meet other Christians and invite them to join us."

Students met others whom they didn't know were Christians. They made plans to connect with one another after this event and pray for one another. Later that evening at a Youth for Christ sponsored evening wrap-up for area high school teens, kids took turns sharing their stories about what happened and how God was working in their schools.

Events like these carry a powerful message to the world: God is alive, and he is still working in public schools. He's building future leaders who are learning today how to stand strong against the secular mainstream, how to love and pray for non-Christian friends and teachers. He honors his promises and loves to answer their prayers. God is building strong leaders much like he always has, in unlikely places. Many will come from our public schools today.

One of the students on the radio interview was Kate Stoner, a junior at a large area high school. "You have to be strong in public school," she said recently. "People have asked me questions trying to disprove the Bible. I would go home and be forced to find the answer. You have to be able to defend what you believe. It made me a lot stronger." Adversity often is unwelcome, but it is one of God's best tools for building strength.

Even in the best of circumstances, Christian students like Kate need plenty of encouragement. Behind many of these teenagers are Christian parents or mentors, like the staff members at Youth for Christ, and countless volunteer youth workers around the globe who pray diligently for them every day, check regularly to see how they're doing, lead Bible studies, and plan outrageously fun events, like caving trips, canoe trips, and indoor skateboarding tournaments.

But there will never be a replacement for the Christian home, where a child's faith is born and nurtured, spiritual strength instilled, and character shaped. Parents whose desire is to see their children become all God wants them to be will send them to school well equipped to succeed. That begins in their attitude.

The Most Important School Supply: A Great Attitude

Christian parents sending their children to public school primarily want a healthy learning environment in which their children can bloom and grow, expand their understanding of the world, and explore the abilities God gave them without losing their faith or buying into a distorted worldview. In the process, our children will touch many more lives than their parents in the educational system. It is critical that we help them develop an attitude that's both teachable and pleasing to God.

Parents must aim for an environment at home where their values, faith, and a healthy attitude toward learning are both caught and taught. In Virelle's book *Loving,*

Launching, and Letting Go (Broadman & Holman, 1995), she talks about many of the ways parents can "salt their home" and make their kids hungry for their faith and values, how to build strength into their children through struggles, and draw a circle of safety and closeness around their family that will reduce emotional distance and help kids grow strong. In addition, as parents we need to send our children to school with an attitude that facilitates learning, not necessarily accepting everything they're taught, but a willingness to accept the disciplines that accompany growth. The following nine ways to equip our children to learn are certainly not exclusive, but will provide a healthy beginning.

Nine Ways to Equip Future Leaders for School

- Emphasize reachable but high standards academically.
- Expect courteous, respectful behavior at all times.
- Demonstrate desired behaviors at home and in our "public persona."
- Be supportively involved in homework, but don't do it for them.
- Be actively involved in the local school system.
- Create a climate for confidential, safe discussion at home.
- Pray daily with our children for their teachers and fellow classmates.
- Instill a love of learning at home through reading, stimulating discussions, educational travel, exposure to people from other countries.
- Help them learn to handle challenges with God's help, but also act on their behalf when necessary.

Ken was a teen whose life fell apart when his parents divorced. After moving from place to place with an abusive father, Ken soon ended up with no family and no place to go. A Christian family gave him a place in theirs. His senior-year friends invited him to an after-school Bible study and prayer group. He soon came to Christ and became a stronger Christian than many of the students from Christian homes.

School can be a rocky experience for many kids. When the going gets rough, these three key factors can turn things around.

At least one praying parent, relative, or close friend. Commit yourself to pray for your children, grandchildren, or your friend's children every day, for their teachers, and at least one or two others. Kate prays with her mom every morning in the car en route to school. It's a special time of sharing she looks forward to each day. Her mother, Barbara, prays regularly with a Moms in Touch group for her local school system, especially that Christian teachers and students will become acquainted with one another and encourage each other.

Help is always available. Don't give up and give in to defeat when your children hit a big snag in school. Help is available. Get personally involved in homework by being helpful, not pushy. If that causes too much tension, diffuse it by hiring a tutor. If money is a problem, consider trading services for tutoring. One mother we know cooked dinner for her tutor once a week in exchange for help. Do everything in your power to help your children do well, discover their gifts, and not settle for less than their best.

One clear exception is emotional health. If you see signs of undue anxiety or despondency, frankly, your child's mental and emotional health are far more important than academic achievement. We would advise you to emphasize all your child's strengths, maximize every God-given ability, and de-emphasize school. Until the stress level is reduced, academic achievement will be close to impossible. If needed, seek counseling from a professional you trust. In the long run, no one will ever ask your son or daughter at age thirty how well he or she did in algebra. Character, emotional well-being, and a heart for God are far more important in life.

Meeting God. Steve saw a bumper sticker recently that read, "As long as there are tests, there will be prayer in schools." We both chuckled, but the truth is, problems in school can lead kids to want to know God. Support Christian outreach into your local public schools, such as Youth for Christ, Campus Life, and your church's youth group. Open your home to your children's unchurched friends, feed them, invite them on vacation with you, meet their needs any way you can. Most of all, love them and pray for them to meet God on their own.

Saying "Thank You!"

One family we knew invited their child's favorite teacher home each spring for dinner. The parents made it a special evening, expressing their thanks for the teacher's hard work and the progress he or she had fostered in their child's life. Their children presented their teachers with thank-you gifts of original poetry or artwork related to their school experience that year. It was a wonderful way to convey appreciation and respect for a special teacher and, no doubt, carried a big message back to the school: These parents care and so do their children!

Our family has expressed appreciation over the years to favorite teachers, too. When our son Dave and his buddies graduated from high school, several of the boys had the idea of honoring the fourth-grade teacher they had all loved with a dinner at our house. Mrs. Franklin is an imposing woman with a winning smile, commanding presence, and an unflinching belief that her students are positively gifted. She loves her students fiercely, rewards their efforts publicly, never accepts shoddy work, and builds them up to want to achieve their best. One of David's friends wrote his college entrance essay about her influence on his life, the way she believed in him when no one else did. Three of our four children have passed under Mrs. Franklin's eagle eye and brilliant teaching. She prepared them well for success in the challenging years of middle school that lay ahead.

On the evening of the dinner party to honor her, Mrs. Franklin's eyes teared first with emotion when her former students presented her with flowers and their thanks, followed quickly by tears of happiness and shrieks of laughter with their collection of funny stories from her classroom.

The point is: Children learn from their parents how to say thank you. They learn to pray for their teachers, show them respect, work hard, and live out their faith the best that they can. Great teachers who also give the best that they can deserve to be thanked.

What about Kids from Tough Circumstances?

Do you worry that your particular home life isn't good enough to grow a future leader? Take heart. Kids don't have to come from "the right side of the tracks" or an exemplary two-parent Christian home to grow up straight and strong. Quite the contrary, some of the most accomplished people have come from very unlikely circumstances. Youth for Christ staff member Brian Bateman shared this moving story with me about a former student in his group:

> Doug was the youngest of three boys from a single-parent family. Both older brothers repeatedly got into trouble with the law, one even ended up in prison. Doug was a shy, timid junior high student when I met him, but he had a real hunger for God. I could tell he appreciated the attention when I tried to mentor him, but he was so shy it was like feeding a squirrel.
>
> When Doug was in ninth grade, he became friends with another boy, one year older, who was his exact opposite—extroverted and the class

clown. Mike was a rebel from a Christian home, always into trouble, smoking, doing drugs, breaking into places for fun, but in ninth grade he went on a mission trip and surrendered his life to God. He began to use his mold-breaking zeal for Jesus.

Since Mike is one year older than Doug, when he and Doug became best friends, it did a lot for Doug's personality. But the big changing point in his life came the summer after ninth grade, when both boys went on a Youth for Christ mission trip to Albania for two months working in medical missions accompanying a doctor and a dentist. The stories they told later were incredible. Since there had been no dentists in Albania for fifty years, people would stand in line to have their teeth pulled with no anesthesia. Doug was one of the few with a strong enough stomach to stand it. Soon he felt God's call into medical missions.

Doug is presently in his second year of medical school with the intention of becoming a missionary. His friend Mike felt a similar call to missions. He became an itinerant preacher, who traveled to over sixteen countries and is now working to organize a teen missions group in Europe. These two guys were filled with zeal; they saw no boundaries.

Doug and Mike have remained lifetime friends. Doug once said to me, "The reason we were able to do this is because you believed in us." I had confidence that God would use them. It showed me how casting your vision into kids really can help shape their lives.

Can God take care of our children in public school? Can he use them to reach others for Christ and bless the world? He can, and he does.

Chapter Highlights

- The most important school supply: a great attitude
- Nine ways to equip future leaders for school
- Three things that make the difference
- Saying "thank you!"
- What about kids from tough circumstances?

Key Thought

God is alive, and he is still working in public schools. He's building future leaders who are learning today how to stand strong against the secular mainstream, how to love and pray for non-Christian friends and teachers. He honors his promises and loves to answer their prayers. God is building strong leaders much like he always has, in unlikely places. Many will come from our public schools today.

What You Can Do

1. Check the lines of communication at home. Make it your aim to talk regularly, openly, and with a determination to listen well to your child when he or she comes home from school.
2. Do you supervise homework, offering constructive suggestions rather than criticism? Do you define reachable standards and demonstrate a love of reading and learning at home?
3. Enhance the environment for learning by turning off the TV or any distracting music during study hours. Be available for help without "hovering" over your child.
4. Pray for your child and his friends and teachers daily. Encourage his faith by making regular attendance at youth ministry functions, such as Youth for Christ or your church youth group, possible. Offer to carpool his friends.

Chapter Thirteen

The Best School in Town Creating a Vision

Once a teacher was working on a "Mission Statement" project, through shared decision making, with me and had to call me at home. He recently had his second child and after our business was done, he quietly asked me when I started taking our son to church, because he was truly different than everyone else. I had the opportunity to tell him where I went to church and about God. **Christyne Kucera, parent volunteer**

Call to me and I will answer you and tell you great and unsearchable things you do not know. **Jeremiah 33:3**

The first time we attended a Family Life marriage conference, we learned about God's blueprint for marriage in a colorful way through the teaching and example of several couples who came to speak. They drew a wonderful picture of marriage the way God intended it to be, and it became the model for our own marriage. Now, over twenty years later, we are excited about attending the first Family Life conference in our own area.

Wouldn't it be wonderful if there were as clear a blueprint for schools? Nevertheless, educators work hard to envision schools as they could be and then attempt to follow their plans, much like an architect follows a blueprint. It's called "visioning," the process of defining the desired outcome and deciding which road is best to take you there. Experts spend a lot of time creating a vision of schools of the future. Shared decision making offers you a voice in the process. The input of Christian parents and educators is critically needed to help create new visions of effective schools with character.

Creating a Blueprint

In his book *Reinventing Education,* Louis Gerstner, CEO of IBM, recommends what he believes is the best way to get the job done, outlining a vision of new schools.

Certain features of school improvement will show up over and over again in the stories told by school principals and teachers, by parents and administrators. In virtually every successful school, foreign visitors will find five things:

- a dynamic, communicative principal, with great freedom to lead his or her school toward a vision of educational excellence;
- a rigorous set of school goals, and a system in place for measuring progress toward them;
- a cadre of competent teachers, whose enthusiasm is multiplied by their use of many advanced education tools and technologies;
- students who are workers—engaged, enthusiastic, and hard-working; and
- an engaged group of parents, supported by a vigorous program that directly involves them in the school.

What actions must be taken to make these things happen, and who must take them?

Nothing matters more for the future of American public schools than finding great principals to lead them.[1]

Great Leadership and a Healthy Moral Climate

What a wonderful opportunity for Christian principals who are highly educated, well informed, networked, and very moral. Gerstner believes that leaders must provide a climate that nurtures the development of a shared vision. What do we mean by vision or shared vision? One of the most creative expressions or visions of tomorrow's schools will be found in "Images of Potential," a short but provocative document produced by the National Foundation for the Improvement of Education (NFIE). This organization brought thirty-eight professionals together for a two-day working conference. Their charge was to develop scenarios or images of technology-rich school learning environments, something you can help your schools do as they plan your child's education.

The NFIE group developed six complete scenarios or visions for different types of schools, such as "rural elementary school" and "urban/suburban high school." Each scenario or vision was expressed in narrative form like a story. For example, the first scenario for the rural elementary school began like this:

It is the turn of the twenty-first century and Ms. Harrison is returning to her home town where she has just signed her first-year teaching contract. Ms. Harrison is the pride of the community, since she is one of the local American Indians who went to college and is serious about sharing the benefits she has gained from her educational opportunities.

She remembers fifth grade, because that was the year she decided to become a teacher. Her grandparents lived on the reservation, but Suzy, as they called her then, lived with her parents in town. Her father worked in the oil field and her mother as a clerk in one of the local stores. Both of her parents valued her in-school education but were concerned that she was not developing an understanding of her cultural heritage. Her grandmother shared this concern.

The school's technology aided her in developing an oral history of her family's tribe. The school's resources included a computer lab with a modest number of computers, as well as a satellite dish, VCRs, overhead projectors, and a library. Suzy checked out a tape recorder and instamatic camera to record the data she gathered from her grandmother and other older women in the tribe.[2]

Suzy's scenario continues to develop and describe how she went on to college, became very proficient with all aspects of technology, and how she actually brought about significant change both in her schools as a teacher and in her community as a technology specialist.

The complete scenarios or visions of the future that the NFIE team produced are very creative and make the reader want to see them come to life. That's the kind of new school vision you want your children to experience. For more detailed information regarding the process your district can use to develop their vision of schooling for the twenty-first century, refer them to page 181 in the endnotes, which provides an outline of the process used by NFIE.[3]

Developing a Shared Vision

When concerned people get together and share their personal visions for new schools, a shared vision begins to emerge. Peter Senge, author of *The Fifth Discipline: The Art & Practice of the Learning Organization*, describes a shared vision:

At its simplest level, a shared vision is the answer to the question, "What do we want to create?" Just as personal visions are pictures or images people carry in their heads and hearts, so too are shared visions pictures that people throughout an organization carry. They create a sense of commonality that permeates the organization and gives coherence to diverse activities.[4]

Creating the vision together motivates parents, teachers, and administrators to action so that over time, the proposed vision becomes real. That's not only fun; it's very rewarding. Make sure you get involved in your district's strategic planning, and encourage leaders to envision new learning environments that will capture students' minds.

Bringing out the Best in America's Schools

Now that you have a better idea of what your school can become and the importance of a shared vision of the future, it is time to envision a school that would come closest to our ideal. It should be unique, inspiring, and values-based, and rest on the solid foundation of a Judeo-Christian worldview.

William Bennett, author of *The De-Valuing of America*, acknowledges the role of religion in the curriculum of our schools:

> In too many places in American public education, religion has been ignored, banned, or shunned in ways that serve neither knowledge, nor the Constitution, nor sound public policy. There is no good curricular or constitutional reason for textbooks to ignore, as many do, the role of religion in the founding of this country or its prominent place in the lives of many of its citizens. We should acknowledge that religion—from the Pilgrims to the civil rights struggle—is an important part of our history, civics, literature, art, music, poetry, and politics, and we should insist that our schools tell the truth about it.[5]

All of this should result in a healthy resurgence of truth, sound values, and character education. We will eventually produce graduates once again with a conscience who embrace democracy and reach for high academic standards.

It would be naive to think that all public schools in America would embrace this vision of the future. Some won't, but we can begin to create a wholesome vision for new schools that will positively affect our society. If we don't act quickly, the pagan model will saturate schools completely.

Bennett, at the end of *The De-Valuing of America*, expresses his deep concern for the controlling influence of others on our public schools:

Those whose beliefs govern our institutions will in large measure win the battle for the culture. And whoever wins the battle for the culture gets to teach the children. This cultural and institutional reclamation project will not be easy.

So be it. Reclaiming our institutions is less a political opportunity than a civic obligation. It involves hard work. But it is a work of immense importance. At the end of the day, somebody's values will prevail.[6]

You don't want just anyone's values to prevail at the end of the school day; you want your values to prevail. Briefly, then, the following are three elements of a great public school environment.

A Culture of Learning

Picture a school managed by leaders of high integrity and character, openness, and strong Judeo-Christian beliefs and values. These leaders will help the community develop a shared vision of what their schools could become and develop strategies to see that this vision is brought to reality. Accountability measures will be implemented to track improvement over time as the vision is realized. Research has proven that great principals motivate schools to accomplish extraordinary results, including the realization of shared visions.

Our school leaders will not forget the importance of celebration and its impact on moral values. We've lost our sense of community because community involves relationships, ritual, and memories of events and accomplishments. These elements come together with great emotional impact during ceremonies. William Kilpatrick shares the importance of celebrating accomplishment:

Although they are often considered extraneous to the real business of school, rituals and ceremonies are among the most effective ways of impressing students with the significance of values held in common. Graduation ceremonies are a prime example. Among other things, they signify the importance of learning, and the value placed on it by the community.[7]

Our schools will exude an enthusiasm for learning that is contagious. As students enter school each day, they will be greeted by enthusiastic principals, teachers, and supporting staff. School personnel will model a love of learning and convey a sense of anticipating success for each child. Nothing great was ever accomplished without passion and enthusiasm. When both are present, students are highly motivated and achieve beyond all expectations.

A wholesome learning environment is nurtured by a student's surroundings. Are the walls of the school decorated with students' writing and art work? Are classrooms filled with interest centers that pique a student's curiosity? Is music being used that inspires positive emotions in students? Kilpatrick believes music "has powers to go far beyond entertainment. It can play a positive role in moral development by creating sensual attractions to goodness, or it can play a destructive role by setting children on a temperamental path that leads away from virtue."[8] Quality music must be encouraged in our new schools, perhaps it could even be played softly all day long in the halls.

A culture of learning without laughter is antithetical. Humor is an amazing teacher. It's been said of A. W. Tozer that there were times when he could hardly finish a sermon because of the laughter in the audience. What great teaching! Roland Barth believes that "humor, like risk taking and diversity, is highly related to learning and the development of intelligence, not to mention quality of life. And humor can be a glue that binds an assorted group of individuals into a community. People learn and grow and survive through humor. We should make an effort to elicit and cultivate it, rather than ignore, thwart, or merely tolerate it."[9]

The culture of learning in our schools will rest on the foundations of character and integrity. We want our children graduating with value-laden habits of living based on respect and responsibility. We want children to be courageous, honest, self-confident, dependable, hard-working, getting good grades, amiable, good-tempered, sensitive to others, and eager to learn. Graduating students with high academic achievement while knowing right from wrong will make a major contribution to the future of America.

A Learning Community

Our schools will reflect often on the quality of the learning environment designed for students and make continuous improvements until the desired vision is achieved.

A great way to think about the meaning of TEAM is "Together Everyone Achieves More." A learning community, like Peter Senge's learning organization, can continually expand "its capacity to create its future. Real learning gets to the heart of what it means to be human. Through learning we re-create ourselves. Through learning we become able to do something we never were able to do. Through learning we reperceive the world and our relationship to it."[10]

Parents, school personnel, and community members working together will envision and realize schools that get better and better as the years go by. They will pay close attention to high academic standards, discipline, and character, much like parochial schools have been doing for many years.

In order for our schools to become learning communities, there will be a mutual commitment to expand open, honest, transparent, and nonthreatening communication. Learning organizations die from lack of communication. Like families, they languish with poor communication but thrive on proactive, problem-solving communication. School issues and problems must be solved quickly, reasonably, and fairly.

A Solid System

A good organization or company has a profound effect on the individuals within it. In similar ways, systemic school reform at the state, district, and building levels will influence teachers and their students. Our vision of schooling in America will benefit from those elements of systemic school reform emphasizing high standards for academic achievement and difficult, high-quality exams to determine success.

Systemic reform can focus resources on building capacity at the local level so that all schools and all children reach their full potential. Choice of schools will be possible within this reform model, especially when students are not achieving the desired learning standards.

The power of a coherent vision of school reform happens when clearly articulated relationships among curriculum, instruction, and assessment are carefully aligned. Then every lesson a student experiences throughout his school career contributes to higher levels of academic achievement and moral development. A strong system will hold alignment steady.

Technology applications and staff development for teachers, administrators, and parents will be on the "front burner" of our school-improvement agenda. No school designed to shape America's future can renew itself without advanced technology and solid professional development programs. We must continue to prepare students for the information age and the knowledge industry it has spawned. Both colleges and industry expect high school graduates to be very comfortable with the new technologies.

Our new American schools will shape the future of our country by graduating world-class students who practice right living. They will lead our country to the new millennium inspired by quality literature, music, art, and core academic subjects.

Some will choose to serve their nation in the military, government, teaching, and professional fields. Others will choose service industries, agriculture, business, and free enterprise.

Above all else, many families and their children, teachers and administrators, board members and committee members, office staff, custodians, and bus drivers will come to know Jesus Christ as their personal Savior and Lord because you and your children were salt and light in the public schools. May God bless your efforts to reach out to our schools. You are touching the future of America.

Chapter Highlights

- Creating a blueprint
- Great leadership and a healthy moral climate
- Developing a shared vision
- Bringing out the best in America's schools
- A culture of learning
- A learning community
- A solid system

Key Thought

It would be naive to think that all public schools in America would embrace this vision of the future. Some won't, but we can begin to create a wholesome vision for new schools that will positively affect our society. If we don't act quickly, the pagan model will saturate schools completely.

What You Can Do

1. Call your state education department, tell them the school district you are in, and ask them if there is a top-notch school or school district that you could visit in the vicinity. They should be able to lead you in the right direction or to the right information that can help you decide what school to visit. Top-notch schools will be different from average schools; you'll be able to see and almost feel the differences. Trips to other schools or districts can give you great insights into helping your own district.

2. Call 1-800-USA-LEARNS and ask to be placed on the mailing list for the Department of Education's community newsletter. This monthly publication lists

many helpful initiatives throughout the country, including teleconferences that you might be able to participate in within your community or state. Other useful resources are listed in this helpful publication.

3. Call your district offices and ask for a copy of the master plan for school improvement or the district's strategic plan for school reform. If they do not have one, see if you can become a parent representative on a new committee designed to develop such a plan.

Chapter Fourteen

Getting There Salting the Vision for America's Schools

We should not all be separatists—running off to "do our own thing." That doesn't help those left behind. The salt must be mixed in to affect the whole. The light must shine in the darkness. **Linda Thompson, middle school science teacher**

You are the salt of the earth. But if the salt loses its saltiness, how can it be made salty again? It is no longer good for anything, except to be thrown out and trampled by men. **Matthew 5:13**

It was the end of a long day, in fact, a long year of endless meetings for the vision-casting committee at school. It had been difficult at first gaining the trust and respect of the teachers, administrators, and fellow committee members, but in time Stuart had established a rapport with most of them. In fact, he'd been convinced by Christians in his town to run for school board election, which seemed an impossible task in his increasingly liberal community. It had been a tough race, culminating in a radio interview and television appearance on election day.

He came home late that evening wishing his wife, Katie, were asleep. He hated telling her the news. Instead, there she was, waiting up for him again.

"How'd it go?" she asked. "I've been praying all evening and so have our kids. They each called."

"Not too bad. How did I look on TV?"

"A little tired and middle aged, but still handsome as ever; now get to the point!"

"Well, I lost the vote to be on the board. The votes were all recounted around ten, and I lost by a small margin. I'm sorry to let you down. But one good thing did happen!" Stuart brightened. "The superintendent said he really valued my contributions and team-building abilities this past year on the Vision Committee and asked me to head up the planning for a districtwide character education program. I think I can do that pretty well, and I agreed. Was that OK with you?"

"Oh, honey! I'm so proud of you! You have so much to offer in that area. Nobody could do it better! I'm not disappointed at all that you lost. I know you'll have just as good an affect in this capacity for now. The Lord knows where you are needed most. Wait until we tell the kids. They'll ask if you'll be using all those funny pieces of cardboard you used to teach them at the dinner table! Promise me you won't do that!"

"I promise. Tell them we need them to pray. I have the feeling God wants me in the place of the most critical need, and right now, that's with shaping our children's character. Choosing the right program won't be easy. You know, tomorrow I'm going to call some folk I think would be great on this committee! But right now, I'm exhausted! Let's get some sleep."

And so it happens across America. Stuart and Katie really live in every community. You know them, too. They are the ones who have seen the gaping needs of their local school and brought it to God, saying, "What do you want me to do here?"

God always places his willing children where they can serve him best, where they will be salt, where they can preserve, and heal, and infuse health back into the homes, families, and schools within their communities. He equips them, as he always does for any task, with knowledge, wisdom, and discernment and the powerful weapon of prayer. Are you ready to ask, "Lord, what do you want *me* to do?"

This final chapter offers you a plan to help you begin. It is the beginning of your vision of the future for American schools.

What Have We Learned?

First, let's take a look at what we've learned so far. One of the most important factors affecting our schools is the culture of learning, often completely unique in every community. As you look at your own school, is it a learning community where everyone values achievement and accomplishment, or is it more a place for children to go during the day, with real learning taking place at home in front of the TV?

Many students find schools so unreal that they can't even relate to them. Why is this happening? Are America's children too "soft," coddled with all the comforts our country has grown to consider normal? This, coupled with a growing lack of discipline at home, explains a lot of poor performance. Schools' needs are symptomatic of far bigger needs within the family.

Hot issues will never go away because they collide with people's differing values and beliefs. Until school districts come to consensus on shared vision, values, beliefs, and worldview, hot issues will continue to erupt. We must learn to deal with these issues without destroying our schools, embarrassing our children, and driving others from Christ. The spiritual battle continues.

One Size Never Fits All

The number of reform efforts throughout the country is astounding, with each approach having a particular flavor and group of supporters. In actuality, success is aided by diversity of opinion and an innovative spirit. We should encourage research into proven practices and support teachers who are trying to help all students to higher levels of achievement.

However, before innovations are adapted "whole hog," they should have some proof of their effectiveness with students similar to those in your district. All innovation isn't bad; some is validated and has been proven effective. For years, the National Diffusion Network disseminated information on validated practices that schools can adapt for their purposes. Within states, there has been an increase in sharing among school districts of programs that really work. States are also disseminating more "promising practices." These programs have a level of validity that puts them in a class way beyond hearsay.

With the continued expansion of the World Wide Web, we will see a rapid increase in information on "promising practices" and related research. The World Wide Web will help school districts be more discerning before deciding to adapt certain techniques or programs.

Schooling in America is very complex, bureaucratic, and highly resistant to change. From a national perspective, systemic school reform is well underway. Federal officals set standards, encourage states to reach these standards (or lose funding), and develop national tests to keep track of student achievement across every state. Although systemic reform has redeeming attributes, federal involvement, especially national testing, flies in the face of the state's responsibility for public schooling.

If we've learned anything, we've learned that the schools our children attend are as good as the community demands or as bad as the community allows. There is an evident relationship between the quality of life in a community and its schools. If a neighborhood starts to deteriorate, it's likely the schools will follow suit.

Moral deterioration is another related concern. Early in our nation's history, children's schooling reinforced commonly held family values. Spelling and reading lessons were based on the Bible and other classical texts, providing all schools with a common moral foundation that spread throughout society. Schooling, families, and society reinforced the same values. That's an unbeatable combination that no longer exists, but must be reclaimed.

Fortunately, there is a growing recognition of the shallowness of morality in our schools, families, and society. It is a sad state of affairs when taxes pay for abortions and newer, larger jails, and when we can read a Bible in jail but not in school.

We believe America has reached its limit of tolerance for bad behavior, crime, drugs, free sex, and other amoral activities. We believe the pendulum of social change is swinging away from the left toward a more balanced, conservative center. And we believe that swing will continue through the turn of the century. Examine the evidence. It may be small, but it's encouraging.

- We're tired of crime. The mayor of New York City is cracking down on crime in Manhattan. People living and working there are beginning to feel safe again.
- Teaching abstinence in schools is increasing. Our nation's capital has approved spending millions of dollars on abstinence-based health education programs in schools throughout the country.
- Supreme Court Justice Scalia has clearly and boldly expressed his faith in God and the effect it has on his decisions.
- Michigan legislators have approved statements acknowledging God and his favor and guidance in their state.
- The number of state-level family policy councils has been steadily increasing over the last ten years. They are now operating in thirty-nine states! These conservative organizations promote pro-family legislation and are based on the successful strategies used by the Washington-based Family Research Council. These state-level policy councils operate through "principled persuasion" and have gained considerable influence over the years.
- Professionals in education, such as William Bennett, Thomas Lickona, the late Ernest Boyer, and others have strongly advocated a return to virtues and character education in our schools. They, too, sense the lack of direction in America and want our public schools to be involved in a turnaround from this bad state of affairs.

- A small start, perhaps, but TV and movie producers seem more willing to rate their shows and movies so kids are not inadvertently exposed to indecent programming. But much remains to be done in the world of entertainment and its powerful affect on our young. It has insidious power to define our culture and self-worth.
- Professional organizations for Christian administrators and teachers are on the rise as well as advocacy groups that watch the field of education, such as The Eagle Forum and Wall Builders. We believe the number and strength of these organizations will increase until the pendulum of social change swings to a more balanced center.
- Every time a new school choice option becomes available, most families will benefit, especially Christians. These choice options will bring about changes in the way education is managed, and they will put pressure on public schools to be more responsive to their communities. Expect charter school legislation in all states by the turn of the century. Christians should take full advantage of this opportunity to help envision and create new schools that reflect their values, beliefs, and worldview.
- Legislation has been and will continue to be passed allowing students to participate in "moments of silence" at the beginning of each school day. Although it is far from school prayer, it is a positive move that may better serve Christians. It undoubtedly will induce opportunities to talk about one's faith and beliefs.
- There is more support for teaching both creationism and evolution in our schools. We know of Christian science teachers who present both explanations of the origins of life. Pray for an increase in their numbers. Evolutionists are finally feeling the pressure.
- Even the federal government and President Clinton have tried to clarify the positive role that religion can play in schools. Local school boards and superintendents have been fearful and reactionary in this area, but they do not have state or federal support for these negative positions. A very helpful report titled *Common Ground* from the Freedom Forum clarifies the positive role religion can have in the education of our children. See Resources section for complete information on this report.

You can see by this very cursory list that positive trends are up. We must take advantage of these trends and maximize our:

- knowledge and
- networking for
- positive change.

Networking at Its Best

Is it easy to learn about the culture of learning in our schools? No, because schools are naturally resistant to outside influence. Don't think of this as necessarily bad; their natural resistance can be positive. It protects our children from every "wind of educational change." We are thankful our children went to schools that handled change relatively well. However, our district did buy into several major, ineffective innovations in language arts and mathematics.

Networking can put school improvement on the front burner, but it cannot be done without positive forms of communication. Your ability to influence schools will be related to the quality of your communications, attitude, and commitment. Do you first seek to understand, then to be understood, as Stephen Covey recommends? Commitment means keeping your promises. Are you a promise keeper? When you say you'll do something, do you do it, no matter what happens?

Attitudes reveal a person's beliefs, values, and worldview. They have the same effect as body language. Some psychologists believe that attitude and body language communicate more clearly, dare we say truthfully, than words. For example, how do you feel when you are trying to communicate with a scowling person with his arms crossed?

In order to be effective in your communities, first check your attitude and motive. If you get a green light on these, then pray, study, think, and reflect before speaking, keeping the health and well-being of the entire community in mind, not just your own family. And learn to "mix it up" with nonbelievers. Christ was truly in the world but not of it. In that way he had his greatest influence and so will you.

How to Get the Schools We Need

How do you get what you want? Or better yet, how do you get what you need? It is true that God has promised to supply all our needs, and at times, he gives us our wants and desires as well. If you believe that God does have a plan for your life, how do you move forward with that plan? You don't, unless you step out in faith.

God won't steer a ship in dry dock. Dr. Bob Cook used to say during his radio program, "Faith is taking action based on God's promises." What actions can schools take to improve themselves, and how can you help in God-honoring ways?

Let's Get Sailing!

Prayer is the Christian's lifeblood. It's been said that prayer clears Satan's forces right off the battlefield. Without it, no battles will be won for him. Pray for your child's teachers. Pray for the administrators who are trying to bring about positive change in your schools. Pray for school board members who may not share your worldview. And pray for other parents who are not as involved with their children and schools as they should be. Prayer sets the stage for great things to happen.

Next, continue to seek information and research on educational reform and innovation. This will help you develop a knowledge base and vocabulary that will let you communicate effectively with educators. Educators pride themselves in being "research based." Interestingly, their research base may be very insensitive to Judeo-Christian principles. Keep this in mind when you read about the educational research your school uses to justify its policies, actions, or programs.

Prayerfully decide how to approach your school district. If you have children, be sure to get to know their teachers. If not, start attending board meetings and just listen for awhile. Once you have been to a few board meetings, believe us when we say that those who perceive themselves to be in control will know who you are and will want to know what you are up to.

If they don't introduce themselves to you at board meetings, call the superintendent and explain that you are interested in volunteering as a parent representative on committees. The important committees would include: 1) budget; 2) comprehensive school improvement planning; 3) library or curriculum; 4) assessment; 5) technology; 6) staff development; 7) character education; and 8) new construction. Any one of these committees will give you valuable experience in how the district operates.

Once you have established yourself as a person who truly cares about school quality, continue to relate to more and more teachers and administrators until you get a sense of their basic worldview, or their strongest beliefs and values about education and community. If you sense a commonality, your involvement will continue smoothly. If there is a large discrepancy with your worldview, moral values, or beliefs, be aware but don't give up. You are now beginning to salt your schools.

If you really believe that your schools need significant improvement, document your concerns (e.g., moral values, academics, sex and drug education, concerns of teachers and/or parents) and ask to meet with the superintendent. During this meeting, keep an open mind and let him or her know of your concerns. If the majority in your community has similar concerns, your work will be half done. If not, the superintendent will tell you that the schools cannot respond to every parent's concerns or to every group that seeks influence.

If the superintendent is beginning to end your appointment, there is one more question you must ask, and every superintendent we know will politely respond. The question is: "How do you go about planning for change and improving student achievement in our district?" He may respond with another question, such as, "Do you mean the strategic plan for the district?" or "Do you mean our curriculum development plan?" Now you've got his attention because superintendents pride themselves in leadership, and true leaders must know where they are going and how to pilot the ship of schooling to that destination. If he is at all interested in responding to the question of strategic planning, your foot is in the door and your adventure with school reform is about to begin.

Starting Your Vision Voyage

Vision and the process of "visioning" seem a bit out of the ordinary, but they capture the essence of growth and renewal so well they can't be ignored in school reform efforts. A helpful definition of vision is offered by Kouzes and Posner:

> We prefer vision, first of all, because it is a "see" word. It evokes images and pictures. Second, vision suggests a future orientation—a vision is an image of the future. Third, vision connotes a standard of excellence, an ideal. It implies a choice of values. Fourth, it also has the quality of uniqueness. Therefore, we define a vision as an ideal and unique image of the future.[1]

What gets a district sailing into a new future with energy, resolve, and resilience? Is it charismatic leadership? simply money? federal and state pressure? Perhaps a little of each, but the development of a shared vision of the future is *the one best way* to bring about the changes a community strongly desires, especially a vision that reflects common beliefs and values. It is a slow process, but it will result in a learning community that navigates well until its shared vision is realized. You will help your district attain extraordinary accomplishments by encouraging the superintendent or principal to include the community in the development of a shared vision of high quality schooling in your district.

The energy to move a district forward is generated by the gap between the district's shared vision or desired state and current reality. Peter Senge emphasizes the power of a shared vision:

> A shared vision is not an idea. It is not even an important idea such as freedom. It is, rather, a force in people's hearts, a force of impressive

power. . . . It is palpable. People begin to see it as if it exists. Few, if any, forces in human affairs are as powerful as shared vision.[2]

"Where there is no vision, the people perish." Most of us are familiar with this biblical quote from Proverbs. It packs more wisdom and energy than we'll ever know.

Because so much power is released from a shared vision, it really doesn't matter how long it takes to develop. The community's vision will include what its people believe in and value, the knowledge and skills students will acquire, and the strategies needed to bring about a cultural learning that is sensitive to both students and parents. America's schools will be renewed one building at a time.

By now, you're probably wondering whether you should take that first step to bring salt and light back into America's public schools. How could one person possibly have any effect on a multi-billion-dollar enterprise that touches the lives of millions of children every school day?

Take the next step and trust God to do the rest. He will guide you all the way. Be bold for him and the children of America. Small steps by those with great vision can change the world.

Mother Teresa left her teaching order in India over fifty years ago with nothing but a sari and two rupees. She had a vision of helping the poorest of the poor, the destitute, the diseased, and the dying. With God's help, her dreams were realized, many were loved and cared for, and her name is known the world over. She established more than 550 hospices, convents, and homes in 120 countries. She started religious orders, including 4,500 sisters and 500 brothers. One person, small steps, and a great God of power, mercy, and love.

The same strength, vision, and love can be yours. God is the same yesterday, today, and tomorrow. He'll always be there to encourage you on. May he bless every step you take on your quest to get the best out of America's public schools!

Chapter Highlights

- What have we learned?
- One size never fits all
- Networking at its best
- How to get the schools we need
- Let's get sailing!
- Starting your vision voyage

Key Thought

Hot issues will never go away because they collide with people's differing values and beliefs. Until school districts come to consensus on shared vision, values, beliefs, and worldview, hot issues will continue to erupt. We must learn to deal with these issues without destroying our schools, embarrassing our children, and driving others from Christ. The spiritual battle continues.

What You Can Do

1. Organize a monthly prayer time with the other Christian parents in your school district. Pray specifically for principals and teachers. Pray that plans being made to improve your schools will reflect Judeo-Christian values and beliefs. You also can discuss "next steps" you might take in learning more about school improvement efforts in your district.

2. Contact your local Christian radio station and ask them if they have programming scheduled on public schooling. If not, encourage them to consider this and suggest interviews or discussion formats with knowledgeable Christian educators and authors.

3. Because the moral climate of America's schools has declined so drastically over the last thirty years, contact pastors in the area and encourage them to support continuous prayer for improvements, especially greater consideration of character education for all students.

Notes

Chapter One

1. Thomas Lickona, *Educating for Character* (New York: Bantam Books, 1991), 6–7.

2. William J. Bennett, *The De-Valuing of America* (New York: Simon & Schuster, 1992), 257.

Chapter Two

1. David A. Noebel, *Understanding the Times* (Eugene, Oreg.: Harvest House Publishers, 1991), 23.

2. Quote by James C. Dobson and Gary Bauer taken from David A. Noebel, *Understanding the Times,* 7.

3. Noebel, 8.

4. David W. Smith, *Choosing Your Child's School* (Grand Rapids, Mich.: Zondervan Publishing House, 1991), 77.

5. James C. Dobson, "FPC: Family Policy Councils," a brochure by Focus on the Family, Colorado Springs, Spring 1997.

6. William J. Bennett, *The De-Valuing of America* (New York: Simon & Schuster, 1992), 90.

7. Francis A. Schaeffer, *How Should We Then Live?* (Old Tappan, N.J.: Fleming H. Revell Company), 256.

Chapter Three

1. Linda S. Page, *Pop Quiz: 20 Questions Parents Should Ask Their Child's School* (Colorado Springs: Focus on the Family, 1995), 5.

2. William J. Bennett, *The De-Valuing of America* (New York: Simon & Schuster, 1992), 90.

3. Rebecca Manley Pippert, *Out of the Saltshaker and into the World* (Downer's Grove, Ill.: Intervarsity Press, 1979), 120.

Chapter Four

1. Stanley M. Elam, Lowell C. Rose, and Alec M. Gallup, "The 6th Annual Phi Delta Kappa Gallup Poll of the Public's Attitudes toward the Public Schools," *Phi Delta Kappan,* September 1994.

2. Thomas Lickona, *Educating for Character* (New York: Bantam Books, 1991), 20.

3. *Webster's Seventh New Collegiate Dictionary* (Springfield, Mass.: G.& C. Merriam Company, 1971).

4. William J. Bennett, *The De-Valuing of America* (New York: Simon & Schuster, 1992), 56.

5. Gary L. Bauer, *Our Hopes Our Dreams* (Colorado Springs: Focus on the Family Publishing, 1996), 96–97.

6. Henry A. Huffman, *A Character Education Program* (Alexandria, Va.: Association for Supervision and Curriculum Development, 1994), 17.

7. "Should Public Schools Teach Character?" *Education Reporter,* December (1996): 4.

Chapter Five

1. Linda S. Page, "OBE: What You Don't Know Could Hurt Your Children," *A Focus on the Family Report* (Colorado Springs: Focus on the Family, 1995), 3.

2. William J. Bennett, "Outcome-Based Education: Summary Remarks by William J. Bennett" (Washington, D.C.: Empower America, May 27, 1993), 1.

3. William Kilpatrick, *Why Johnny Can't Tell Right from Wrong and What We Can Do About It* (New York: Simon & Schuster, 1992), 36.

4. William Murchison, *Reclaiming Morality in America* (Nashville: Thomas Nelson Publishers, 1994), 161.

5. Kilpatrick, 53.

6. David Barton, "What Happened in Education?" A report prepared by Specialty Research Associates, Inc., P. O. Box 397, Aledo, TX, 19–20.

7. Letter from James C. Dobson, president of Focus on the Family, Colorado Springs (May 1995): 5.

8. Diane Ravitch, "A Common Culture," *Educational Leadership*, vol. 49, no. 4 (December 1991/January 1992): 8.

9. Rita Dunn, "The Goals and Track Record of Multicultural Education," *Educational Leadership*, vol. 54, no. 7 (April 1997): 77, also referencing R. Dunn and

S. A. Griggs, *Multiculturalism and Learning Styles: Teaching and Counseling Adolescents* (Westport, Conn.: Praeger Publishers, Inc., 1995).

Chapter Six

1. This worldview is Christ-centered, and when we seek him it will permeate every perception and thought we have, every word we speak, sing, or write, and every action we take. As we learn to trust his plan for the world and his will for our lives, our faith in his love and power provides much-needed stability and gives inexplicable peace and confidence—we already know who wins this critical spiritual battle. As we interact with the school community, we should be loving, because our confidence in God can be intimidating to others. When we take time to think about the big issues in our worldview, our politics will include justice, freedom, and order. Our law, both biblical and natural (God's order and design in the universe). Our ethics (Do actions conform to God's character or not?), absolute, not relative. Economically we believe in the stewardship of property, not socialism or the socialistic redistribution of all wealth. David A. Noebel's *Understanding the Times* will provide a more comprehensive treatment of religious worldview.

2. David A. Noebel, *Understanding the Times* (Eugene, Oreg.: Harvest House Publishers, 1991), 8.

3. Corning City School District, 165 Charles Street, Painted Post, New York, NY 14870, "Statement of Beliefs."

4. Central Square Central School District, Central Square, N.Y.

5. John J. Dunphy, *The Humanist Magazine* (January/February, 1983): 26, as quoted in Brannon Howse, *An Educational Abduction: Do You Know What Your Child Is Being Taught?* (Green Forest, Ark.: New Leaf Press, Inc., 1995), 146.

6. Robert L. Linn and Joan L. Herman, *A Policymaker's Guide to Standards-Led Assessment* (Denver: National Commission of the States, 1997), 1.

7. Ibid., 2.

8. The University of the State of New York, The State Education Department, "Learning Standards in Seven Subject Areas," Albany, N.Y., 1997.

9. Eric Buehrer, *Creating a Positive Public School Experience* (Nashville, Tennessee: Thomas Nelson, Inc., 1984), 153.

10. To give you a feeling for the obvious danger in planning all instruction on constructivism, think about truth and wisdom as you read the following quote from Noddings, a radical constructivist, in the book titled *In Search of Understanding: The Case for the Constructivist Classroom* by Jacqueline and Martin Brooks:

Having accepted the basic constructivist premise, there is no point in looking for foundations or using the language of absolute truth. The constructivist position is really post-epistemological [past the study of the limits and validity of knowledge], and that is why it can be so powerful in inducing new methods of research and teaching. It recognizes the power of the environment to press for adaptation [a la Darwin, no doubt], the temporality [here one day, gone tomorrow] of knowledge, and the existence of multiple selves [probably means people] behaving in consonance with the rules of various subcultures [this could be America from Nodding's perspective].

From Noddings, "Constructivism in Mathematics Education," *Journal for Research in Mathematics Education* vol. 4 (1990): 12, as quoted in Jacqueline Grennon Brooks and Martin G. Brooks, *The Case for Constructivist Classrooms* (Alexandria, Va.: Association for Supervision and Curriculum Development, 1993), 6.

11. The University of the State of New York, The State Education Department, "Learning-Centered Curriculum and Assessment for New York State" (Albany, N.Y., April 1994): 3.

12. Robert J. Marzano, Debra Pickering, and Jay McTighe, *Assessing Student Outcomes: Performance Assessment Using the Dimensions of Learning Model* (Alexandria, Va: Association for Supervision and Curriculum Development, 1993), 5.

13. Mike Rose, "What We Talk About When We Talk About School," *Education Week,* vol. 26, no. 4 (September 25, 1996): 39.

Chapter Seven

1. Lonnie Harp, "Who's Minding the Children?" *Education Week* (September 28, 1994): 30.

2. Cliff Schimmels, *Parents' Most-Asked Questions About Kids and Schools: A Leading Educator Answers Concerns About Your Children's Education* (Wheaton, Ill.: Victor Books, 1989), 161.

3. Address by U.S. Secretary of Education Richard W. Riley, "State of American Education," 18 Feb. 1997, *Community Update,* no. 45, March 1997, p. 1, U.S. Department of Education. Available: <http://www.ed.gov/G2K/community/97-03.html.>

4. Schimmels, 156.

Chapter Eight

1. Information from speech by President Bill Clinton, "Update—1998 Budget" Discussion List. EDInfo Listserv. Available E-mail: listproc@inet.ed.gov [6 Feb. 1997].

2. Selected from "Quality Counts: A Report Card on the Condition of Public Education," A Supplement to *Education Week* (January 22, 1997): 7.

3. David Barton, *What Happened in Education?* (Aledo, Tex.: Wallbuilders, Inc., 1993), 1–16.

4. Eric A. Hanushek, "Money Might Matter Somewhere: A Response to Hedges, Lane, and Greenwald," *Educational Researcher* (May 1994): 8.

5. Jeff Archer, "More Urban Minorities in Catholic Schools Get to College, Study Says," *Education Week,* vol 16, no. 25 (March 19, 1997): 8.

Chapter Nine

1. Gary L. Bauer, *Our Hopes Our Dreams* (Colorado Springs: Focus on the Family Publishing, 1996), 86.

2. David Elkind, "School and Family in the Postmodern World," *Phi Delta Kappan,* vol. 77, no. 1 (September 1995), 13.

3. Stanley M. Elam, Lowell C. Rose, and Alec M. Gallup, "The 6th Annual Phi Delta Kappan Gallup Poll of the Public's Attitudes toward the Public Schools," *Phi Delta Kappan,* September 1994.

4. National Education Goals Panel, "1996 National Education Goals Report: Executive Summary," U. S. Government Printing Office, Superintendent of Documents, Mail Stop: SSOP, Washington, D.C. ISBN 0-16-048885-0, 2–3.

5. Letter from James C. Dobson, president of Focus on the Family, Colorado Springs (May 1994): 1–4.

6. U.S. Department of Education, "Companion Document: Cross-Cutting Guidance for the Elementary and Secondary Education Act," Washington, D.C. (September 1996): 2.

7. U.S. Department of Education, "Career Preparation Education: A Vital Part of Education Reform," Washington, D.C. (Fall 1996): 3.

8. Ibid., 4.

9. Joe Esposito, "Tangled Web: A Cumulative Report Incorporating Research of Original Documents Concerning 'School-to-Work,'" Tulsa Eagle Forum, P. O. Box 470734, Tulsa, OK 74147-0734 (1996): 29.

10. Deborah Meier, "How Our Schools Could Be," *Phi Delta Kappan*, vol. 76, no. 5 (January 1995): 370.

11. Ibid., 372.

12. Ibid.

13. Ibid.

14. Mark Buechler, "Colloquium: Out on Their Own," *Technos*, vol. 5, no. 3 (Fall 1996): 30.

15. Gregg Vanourek, Bruno V. Manno, and Chester E. Finn Jr., "The False Friends of Charter Schools," *Education Week*, vol. 26, no. 31 (April 30, 1997): 60.

16. Paul Hayford, personal communication, April 1997.

17. "Voucher Advocates Set Up Attack," *American Teacher* (May/June 1997): 6–7.

18. Gerald Tirozzi, "Vouchers: A Questionable Answer to an Unasked Question," *Education Week*, vol. 26, no. 30 (April 23, 1997): 64–65.

19. Jacques Steinberg, "School Choice Program Gets 17,000 Applications," *The New York Times METRO* (April 24, 1997).

20. David A. Squires and Robert D. Kranyik, "The Comer Program: Changing School Culture," *Educational Leadership*, vol. 53, no. 4 (December 1995/January 1996): 30.

21. John O'Neil, "On Lasting School Reform: A Conversation with Ted Sizer," *Educational Leadership*, vol. 52, no. 5 (February 1995): 4.

22. "Schools That Work," *U.S. News & World Report* (October 7, 1996): 58–64.

23. Ibid.

24. Lynn Olson, "Teachers Need Nuts, Bolts of Reforms, Experts Say," *Education Week*, vol. 16, no. 31 (April 30, 1997): 1.

Chapter Ten

1. Peter F. Drucker, *Innovation and Entrepreneurship* (New York: Harper & Row, 1985) as reported in Stanley Pogrow, "Reforming the Wannabe Reformers: Why Education Reforms Almost Always End Up Making Things Worse," *Phi Delta Kappan*, vol. 77, no. 10 (June 1996): 657.

Chapter Eleven

1. C. S. Lewis, *Mere Christianity* (New York: Macmillan, 1943), 55.

2. "Our Side of the Apple," *Schodack Central School Faculty Newsletter* (November 1996).

3. Evelyn Klob, "Math Rejects of the World!" *On the Ridge*, a newsletter of East Ridge Community Church (December 1996): 1.

4. Roy Maynard, "Home Court Advantage," *World* (February 8, 1997): 15.

5. Ibid., 12.

6. William J. Bennett, *The De-Valuing of America* (New York: Simon & Schuster, 1992), 90.

Chapter Thirteen

1. Louis V. Gerstner, *Reinventing Education: Entrepreneurship in America's Public Schools* (New York: Penguin Books, 1994), 256–57.

2. "Images of Potential," National Foundation for the Improvement of Education, 1201 Sixth Street, NW, Washington, D.C., 20036 (1990, est.): 11.

3. "Developing New Pictures," from pages 30 and 31 in "Images of Potential," by the National Foundation for the Improvement of Education (NFIE), describes techniques you can use in your school district to create a new vision of what you would like your schools to look like and become in the future.

> The visioning process needs to continue at all levels. Communities must define their own values and goals for education, keeping in mind that technology may play a part in realizing their aspirations.
>
> The process through which these "Images of Potential" were drawn can be replicated at the state, local, and even school building level. NFIE has facilitated several such processes at various levels and has found that successful scenario building or visioning involves several key components:

- Bring together people with diverse backgrounds, roles, and responsibilities to discuss a common goal or set of concerns. At the school building level, for example, the group may consist of teachers, students, administrators, parents, corporate and community representatives, a politician, etc.
- Find an isolated place protected from outside interruptions where the group can focus on the task.
- Take time to get acquainted and discover what resources each participant brings to the process. Discuss literature you've read, teaching and learning experiences, the nature of your work, etc.
- Spend some time thinking about the constituency group. Who are the students? What are their needs? What other issues and pressures impact them, e.g., social, economic, and political?
- Remove constraints. Strategic planners often are inclined to focus on what can

be done starting today. This approach stifles creativity because we get caught in the parameters of why we can't do something, due to bureaucracy, finances, etc. Instead, the group might try "visioning" the perfect situation without any of the current constraints. Decide first where it is you would like to go, then draw the map to get there.

- Once you have created the vision, take time to consider what you can and cannot change. In the case of education, we know we can't change the American family structures and trends, nor the economy, but we can work with how schools are structured, how other units affect the school, or how teacher education will affect the future. Think about what will make the scenario real. Recognize external constraints, but only after you have defined the internal goals.

- Play with how things work. Don't insist on a linear progression. Strategic plans tend to begin in fits and starts. One technique used well is the story board. Participants brainstorm different episodes they would like to see occur. You can build the bridges between the episodes later. Don't try to write sentence-by-sentence or get too bogged down in details. The group can spend a day drafting an eloquent introduction, leaving little time to construct the meat of the scenario.

- Most importantly, have fun. Make a serious attempt, however, to be open-minded and creative. Stretch, probe, and draft, and then stretch some more. Building scenarios may be more work than you think, but it probably will be more gratifying as well.

4. Peter Senge, *The Fifth Discipline* (New York: Doubleday, 1990), 206.

5. William J. Bennett, *The De-Valuing of America* (New York: Simon & Schuster, 1992), 205.

6. Ibid., 258.

7. William Kilpatrick, *Why Johnny Can't Tell Right from Wrong and What We Can Do About It* (New York: Simon & Schuster, 1992), 232–33.

8. Ibid., 188–89.

9. Roland S. Barth, *Improving Schools from Within* (San Francisco, Calif.: Jossey-Bass Publishers, 1990), 170.

10. Senge, 14.

Chapter Fourteen

1. James M. Kouzes and Barry Z. Posner, *The Leadership Challenge: How to Get Extraordinary Things Done in Organizations* (San Francisco, Calif.: Jossey-Bass Publishers, 1987), 85.

2. Peter Senge, *The Fifth Discipline* (New York: Doubleday, 1990), 206.

Appendix

Estimated Total Public Education Expenditures and Per-Pupil Expenditures, Pre-K–Grade 12, 1996–97 School Year*

*Derived from Table 5 (p. 7) and Table 7 (p. 9) as reported in "Public Elementary and Secondary Education Statistics: School Year 1996–97," National Center for Education Statistics, U.S. Department of Education, Office of Educational Research and Improvement, July 1997, NCES 97–554.

State	Estimated	Per Pupil Expenditure
Alabama	$3.46 (billions)	$4,663.00
Alaska	1.08	8,593.00
Arizona	3.55	4,734.00
Arkansas	1.54	3,373.00
California	30.27	5,469.00
Colorado	3.59	5,337.00
Connecticut	4.47	8,548.00
Delaware	0.78	7,086.00
District of Columbia	0.73	9,204.00

Getting the Best out of Public Schools

State	Estimated	Per Pupil Expenditure
Florida	12.02	5,365.00
Georgia	8.25	6,243.00
Hawaii	0.98	5,210.00
Idaho	1.09	4,445.00
Illinois	12.55	6,397.00
Indiana	5.84	5,928.00
Iowa	2.87	5,696.00
Kansas	2.57	5,520.00
Kentucky	3.56	5,365.00
Louisiana	3.53	4,541.00
Maine	1.32	6,052.00
Maryland	5.32	6,500.00
Massachusetts	7.05	7,530.00
Michigan	11.04	6,642.00
Minnesota	4.98	5,946.00
Mississippi	2.10	4,163.00
Missouri	4.41	4,988.00
Montana	0.88	5,263.00
Nebraska	1.66	5,991.00
Nevada	1.42	5,016.00
New Hampshire	1.25	6,434.00
New Jersey	12.44	10,189.00
New Mexico	2.13	6,430.00

State	Estimated	Per Pupil Expenditure
New York	24.53	8,684.00
North Carolina	6.17	5,141.00
North Dakota	0.58	4,887.00
Ohio	11.00	5,975.00
Oklahoma	3.04	4,900.00
Oregon	3.25	6,038.00
Pennsylvania	13.02	7,204.00
Rhode Island	1.10	7,298.00
South Carolina	3.17	4,890.00
South Dakota	0.67	4,653.00
Tennessee	4.57	5,129.00
Texas	20.94	5,498.00
Utah	1.83	3,834.00
Vermont	0.75	7,068.00
Virginia	6.67	6,088.00
Washington	5.79	5,958.00
West Virginia	1.83	6,015.00
Wisconsin	5.73	6,479.00
Wyoming	0.60	6,024.00

Resources

This resources section is like a tool box. It is designed to provide you with a broad array of documents, publications, newsletters, organizations, and electronic resources on the World Wide Web. Each tool has been chosen to help you in your quest to rebuild America's public schools. Your adventure is more important than you may realize now. Your efforts will affect communities, their families and children, helping them become all God intended they should be.

Glossary[1]

Authentic Assessment. Assessment that both mirrors and measures student performance in "real-world" tasks and situations. For example, to assess authentically a student's ability to problem solve, the student is given a real-world problem and assessed on how he or she goes about solving it.

Benchmark Performances. Examples of performance that serve as a standard against which other papers or performances may be judged. In writing, for example, benchmark performances are selected from actual student essays that are considered to exemplify the quality of a performance level of "1," "2," "3," and so forth.

Content Standards. Narrative descriptions of expected knowledge and abilities that describe what students should know and be able to do.

Criterion-Referenced Assessment. An assessment designed to reveal what a student knows, understands, or can do in relation to specific performance objectives. Criterion-referenced assessments are used to identify student strengths and weaknesses with regard to specific knowledge or skills that are goals of the instructional program.

Curriculum. All the arrangements a school makes for students' learning and development, including the sequence, format, and content of courses; student activities; teaching approaches; books, materials, and resources used; and the way in which teachers and classes are organized, which enable students to reach standards.

Curriculum-Embedded Assessment. An assessment that occurs in connection with an ongoing teaching and learning activity in the classroom. It may be a project, research paper, or other exhibition of performance.

Curriculum Framework. A broad description of the principles, topics, and modes of inquiry or performance in a discipline that provides the basic structure of ideas

---

1. Glossary in "Learning-Centered Curriculum and Assessment for New York State," The University of the State of New York, The State Education Department, Albany, New York, April 1994. Used with permission.

upon which a curriculum is based. A stepping-stone between standards and curriculum. New York State's curriculum frameworks describe knowledge, skill, and understanding to be developed, major themes and questions to be explored, and performance standards to be attained.

Key Competencies. Fundamental skills—both those general to learning and living (such as problem solving, communicating, reasoning) and those particular to given areas of learning (such as observation, description, explanation, and prediction in science).

Key Concepts. Major ideas that help organize facts and experience and define important understandings in a field of study (examples from science: *motion, machine, friction, speed, work*).

Matrix Sampling. Giving portions of an assessment to different, representative samples of students so that no student need take the entire assessment. The scores that are obtained are group rather than individual scores, and are often used to look at the performance of a school, school district, or state.

Norm-Referenced Assessment. An assessment designed to reveal how an individual student's performance or test result ranks or compares to that of an appropriate peer group.

On-Demand Assessment. An assessment that takes place at a predetermined time and place. Traditional tests, SATs, and most final exams are examples of on-demand assessment.

Open-Ended Tasks. The kind of performance required of students when they must generate a solution to a problem or perform a task when there is no single right answer.

Open-Response Tasks. The kind of performance required of students when they are required to generate an answer, rather than select it from among several possible answers, for which there is a single correct response.

Opportunity-to-Learn Standards (OTL). Also called delivery standards. The ability of schools, in terms of resources, to prepare students to meet content and performance standards.

Performance Assessment. Direct, systematic observation and rating of an actual student performance, or samples of performances in which students create a product or a response to a question or task rather than choosing a response from a given list. Examples include essays, oral presentations, actual demonstrations of physical or artistic ability.

Performance Criteria. A description of the characteristics that will be judged for a task. Performance criteria are expressed in a rubric or scoring guide. Anchor papers or benchmark performances may be used to identify each level of competency in the rubric or scoring guide.

Performance Standards. Levels of student achievement in domains of study. Performance standards answer the question, "How good is good enough?"

Regents Goals. Broad statements, adopted by the New York State Board of Regents, of the knowledge, skills, and civic values all students should acquire through their elementary, middle, and secondary schooling.

Reliability. An indication of the consistency of scores across evaluators or over time. An assessment is considered reliable when the same answers receive the same score across all scorers.

Standardized Assessments. Assessments that are administered and scored in exactly the same way for all students. Traditional standardized tests are typically mass-produced and machine-scored and are designed to measure skills and knowledge that are thought to be taught to all students in a fairly standardized way. However, performance assessments can also be standardized if they are administered and scored in the same way for all students. Standardization is an important consideration if comparisons are to be made between scores.

Task (as in "performance task"). A goal-directed assessment exercise. If the task is authentic, it is designed to elicit from students their application of a broad range of knowledge and skills to solve a complex problem.

Validity. An indication of how well an assessment actually measures what it is supposed to measure. A valid assessment measures what it is supposed to measure and not extraneous features.

Character Education Programs

Here is a list of character education programs that the Association of American Educators (AAE) Advisory Board endorses. These programs are fully integrated, public school-approved curriculums that have a proven track record of success.

1. *Values in Action* is a national award-winning schoolwide comprehensive character education program with eighteen years of research and successful implementation. Contact Bureau of Essential Ethics Education, P.O. Box 80208, Ranch Santa Margarita, CA 92688, (800) 229-3455. E-mail: ethicsusa@earthlink.net. Web site: http://home.earthlink.net/~ethicsusa. (K–12)

2. *WiseSkills* is an innovative school program that combines a variety of positive prevention activities into a simple, yet comprehensive, character-building program. Contact WiseSkills Resources, P.O. Box 3213, South Pasadena, CA 91031, (818) 441-7944. Web site: www.cris.com/~wskills. (K–8)

3. *I Can* Achiever Curriculum teaches children not only the ABCs of education, but more importantly the ABCs of life—Attitude, Behavior, and Character. Contact Zig Ziglar Corp., 3330 Earhart Dr., Suite 204, Carrollton, TX 75006, (800) 527-0306. (K–12)

4. *Jefferson Center for Character Education* has two programs: *S.T.A.R.*: Success Through Accepting Responsibility (K–6) and *How To Be Successful* (7–9). Both use the STAR process—Stop, Think, Act, Review as a conflict-resolution and decision-making process. Contact CEO, 2700 E. Foothill Blvd., Suite 302, Pasadena, CA 91107, (818) 792-8130. E-mail: jeffctr@aol.com.

5. Young People's *Lessons in Character* is a complete curriculum for elementary students built around multicultural literature and the "Six Pillars of Character." It is a Character Counts! Coalition project of the Josephson Institute of Ethics. Contact Young People's Press, Inc., 1731 Kettner Blvd., San Diego, CA 92101,

(800) 231-9774. E-mail: youngpeoplespress@compuserve. (K–5, grade 6 being developed)

6. *STARS (Students Taking a Right Stand)* helps students in grades 6–12 refrain from the use of alcohol and other drugs and learn positive living skills through programs of positive peer pressure and caring confrontation. *The Victor Team* program is designed to reach children in their development (K–6) and teach them important skills to prevent drug abuse and other unhealthy behaviors. Contact P.O. Box 22185, Chattanooga, TN 37422-2185, (800) 477-8277.

Additional Character Education Programs

In addition to those mentioned, these character education programs have been reviewed for us by Dr. Lori Wiley, director of the Character Development Foundation. She is a developmental psychologist, specializing in character education, who conducts ongoing workshops for teachers. You may contact her at P.O. Box 4782, Manchester, NH 03108-4782, (603) 472-3063. We are deeply grateful to Dr. Wiley for her assistance.

Ethics Resource Center, 1120 G Street, NW, Suite 200, Washington, DC 20005, Tel: (202) 434-8478, Fax: (202) 737-2227.

Produces video-based programs to help teachers develop and reinforce positive values and character traits in students, including *What Should You Do?: Deciding What's Right*, a program for grades 4–6; and *Not for Sale: Ethics in the American Workplace*, which offers high school students an introduction to the relationship between personal morality, professional responsibility, and business ethics.

Heartwood Institute, 12300 Perry Highway, PA 16090, Tel: (412) 934-1777, Fax: (412) 934-0050.

Fosters moral literacy and ethical judgment by providing an anchor for children in universal virtues common to the world's cultures and traditions: courage, loyalty, justice, respect, hope, honesty, and love are presented in quality read-aloud multicultural stories that touch the heart and develop within the child a strong basis for moral and character development.

Personal Responsibility Education Process [PREP] Network for Educational Development, 13157 Olive Spur Road, St. Louis, MO 63141, Tel: (314) 576-3535, Fax: (314) 576-4996.

Promotes school-business-community partnerships to develop student character, personal responsibility, and achievement. PREP provides over twenty-two public school districts in greater St. Louis with program guidelines, curriculum resources, staff development, and parent training and information on current research, educational practices, and program evaluation.

Quest International, 537 Jones Road, Granville, OH 43023, Tel: (800) 446-2700, Fax: (614) 522-6580.

Promotes family-school-community partnerships to foster positive youth development. Programs include: *Skills for Growing,* which emphasizes life and citizenship skills for grades K–5; and *Skills for Adolescence,* which emphasizes the creation of supportive partnerships for adolescents in areas such as service learning and multicultural understanding.

In addition to this list, many will welcome to the public school arena the *Children of the World/North American School Project Character Education Curriculum,* developed by Director Vernie Schorr. An internationally acclaimed program that helps children develop a conscience driven by character, it is unique in its emphasis on worldview. For more information, contact them at 910 Calle Negocio, Suite 300, San Clemente, CA 92673-6251, Tel: (714) 361-7575, Fax: (714) 361-7579. Web site: http://www.character.com/cotw/.

Abstinence Education

National Association for Abstinence Education, 6201 Leesburg Pike, Suite 404, Falls Church, VA 22044, (703) 532-9459.

Education for Life, 3700 Galley Road, Suite 150, Colorado Springs, CO 80909, (719) 574-7117.

Medical Institute for Sexual Health, P.O. Box 4919, Austin, TX 78765, (800) 892-9484.

Colorado Coalition for Abstinence Education, Inc., 821 17th St., Suite 690, Denver, CO 80202, (303) 298-8520.

True Love Waits, Baptist Sunday School Board, 127 Ninth Avenue, North, Nashville, TN 37234, (800) 588-9248.

Sex Respect, Respect, Inc., P.O. Box 349, Bradley, IL 60915-0349, (815)932-8389.

Best Friends, 2000 N Street NW, Suite 201, Washington, DC 20036, (202) 822-9266.

For an even more complete listing of videos, curricula, and materials, contact the Family Research Council, 801 G Street, NW, Washington, DC 20001, (800) 225-4008, and ask for their booklet, "Moms & Dads: School Survival Guide."

Suggested Readings

Barna, George. *The Power of Vision*. Ventura, Calif.: Regal Books, 1992.

Barton, David. *The Myth of Separation*. Aledo, Tex.: Wallbuilders Press, 1989.

———. *Original Intent*. Aledo, Tex.: Wallbuilders Press, 1996.

Bauer, Gary. *Our Hopes Our Dreams*. Colorado Springs: Focus on the Family, 1996.

Bedley, Gene. *The Big R-Responsibility*. Irvine, Calif.: People Wise Publications, 1985.

———. *How Do You Recognize a Good School When You Walk into One?* Irvine, Calif.: Gene Bedley, 1980.

Bloom, Alan. *The Closing of the American Mind*. New York: Simon & Schuster, 1987.

Buehrer, Eric. *Creating a Positive Public School Experience*. Nashville, Tenn.: Thomas Nelson Publishers, 1994.

———. *The Public Orphanage: How Public Schools Are Making Parents Irrelevant*. Dallas: Word Publishing, 1995.

Bennett, William J. *The De-Valuing of America*. New York: Simon & Schuster, 1992.

———. *The Book of Virtues*. New York: Simon & Schuster, 1993.

Corcoran, John, with Carole C. Carlson. *The Teacher Who Couldn't Read*. Colorado Springs: Focus on the Family, 1994.

Dobson, James C. and Gary L. Bauer. *Children at Risk*. Dallas: Word Publishers, 1990.

Fuller, Cheri. *Helping Your Child Succeed in Public School*. Colorado Springs: Focus on the Family, 1993.

Gerstner, Louis V. *Reinventing Education in America's Public Schools*. New York: Penguin Books, 1994.

Haynes, Charles C. and Oliver Thomas. *Finding Common Ground.* Nashville: The Freedom Forum First Amendment Center, 1994.

Howse, Brannon. *An Educational Abduction.* Green Forest, Arkansas: New Leaf Press, 1993.

Kilpatrick, William. *Why Johnny Can't Tell Right from Wrong and What We Can Do About It.* New York: Simon & Schuster, 1992.

Kouzes, James M. and Barry Z. Posner. *The Leadership Challenge.* San Francisco: Jossey-Bass, Inc., 1987.

Lickona, Thomas. *Educating for Character.* New York: Bantam Books, 1991.

McDowell, Josh. *Right from Wrong.* Dallas: Word Publishing, 1994.

Murchison, William. *Reclaiming Morality in America.* Nashville: Thomas Nelson Publishers, 1994.

Noebel, David. *Understanding the Times.* Eugene, Oreg.: Harvest House Publishers, 1991.

Pippert, Rebecca Manley. *Out of the Salt Shaker and into the World.* Downers Grove, Ill.: Intervarsity Press, 1979.

Schaeffer, Francis. *A Christian Manifesto.* Westchester, Ill.: Crossway Books, 1982.

———. *How Should We Then Live?* Old Tappan, N.J.: Fleming H. Revell Company, 1976.

Schimmels, Cliff. *Parents' Most Asked Questions About Kids and Schools.* Wheaton, Ill.: Victor Books, 1989.

———. *It Is Time for School.* Elgin, Ill.: David C. Cook, 1989.

———. *How to Shape Your Child's Education.* Elgin, Ill.: David C. Cook, 1989.

Smith, David W. *Choosing Your Child's School.* Grand Rapids, Mich.: Zondervan Publishing House, 1991.

Tobias, Cynthia Ulrich. *The Way They Learn.* Colorado Springs: Focus on the Family, 1994.

Whitehead, John. *The Second American Revolution.* Westchester, Ill.: Crossway Books, 1987.

———. *The Rights of Religious Persons in Public Education.* Wheaton, Ill.: Crossway Books, 1994.

Newsletters and Periodicals

"Washington Watch," published by the Family Research Council, 801 G Street, NW, Washington, DC 20001, (202) 393-2100.

"Teachers in Focus" and "Citizen," published by Focus on the Family, P.O. Box 35500, Colorado Springs, CO 80935-3550, (719) 531-5181.

"The Gateways Report," published by Gateways to Better Education (Erich Buehrer), P.O. Box 514, Lake Forest, CA 92630-0514, (714) 586-KIDS.

"Sexual Health Update," published by Medical Institute for Sexual Health (M.I.S.H.) P.O. Box 4919, Austin, TX 78765, (800) 892-9484, E-mail: mish@worldnet.att.net, web site: http://www.mish.org.

"Hands On!" deals with math and science education, published by TERC Communications, 2067 Massachusetts Ave., Cambridge, MA 02140, (617) 547-0430, web site: http://www.terc.edu.

"Facts & Faith," deals with scientific evidence of biblical truth, published quarterly by Reasons to Believe, P.O. Box 5978, Pasadena, CA 91117, (818) 335-1480. E-mail: reasons@reasons.org, web site: http://www.reasons.org.

"Current Thoughts & Trends," summaries of the best Christian and secular periodicals, published by The Navigators, 7899 Lexington Drive, Colorado Springs, CO 80920, (800) 288-2028.

"Wallbuilder Report," published quarterly by Wallbuilder Presentations (David Barton), P.O. Box 397, Aledo, TX 76008-0397, (817) 441-6044.

"Education Reporter," published by Eagle Forum Education and Legal Defense Fund, Box 618, Alton, IL 62002, (618) 462-5415.

"The American Educator," published by the Association of American Educators, 26012 Marguerite Parkway, #333, Mission Viejo, CA 92692, Tel: (800) 704-7799, Fax: (714) 582-0120.

"The Defender," published by the Christian Legal Society, P.O. Box 637, 4208 Evergreen Lane, Suite 222, Annandale, VA 22003-1072, (703) 642-1072.

On-Line Resources

U.S. Department of Education
http://www.ed.gov

Education Resource Organizations Directory,
containing over 1,800 state,
regional and national organizations
http://www.ed.gov/, offices/OPE/PPI/hopehome.html

Family Research Council
http://www.frc.org

Conservative Professional Organizations

Association of American Educators
26012 Marguerite Parkway, Suite 333
Mission Viejo, CA 92692
(800) 798-1124

Christian Educators Association International
P.O. Box 50025
Pasadena, CA 91115
(818) 798-1124

The Case for Parental Involvement in the Schools*

By Linda S. Page, former Manager of Education Policy, Focus on the Family

The most important reason to be actively involved in your children's school(s) is that you as a parent are responsible for your children's education. Current evidence shows that when parents are meaningfully involved in their children's education, scholastic achievement can greatly improve. According to the book, *The Evidence Continues to Grow,* by Anne Henderson, the positive impact of parental involvement "is beyond dispute. . . . Programs designed with strong parental involvement produce students who perform better than otherwise identical programs that do not involve parents as thoroughly, or that do not involve them at all" (p. 1).

The type of parental involvement that makes a positive difference in student achievement is more than "volunteering." While supporting the teacher by helping with school activities such as bake sales, holiday parties, or booster clubs is important, your concerns go deeper than this; and so should your involvement. Parents must become directly involved in their children's academic learning experience.

What You Can Do

Stay well informed about the educational program. Though you may delegate the activity of educating to a school, you still need to know the answers to these questions:

- What skills and information are my children being taught in each subject?

* Used by permission from Focus on the Family.

- How much time is spent on core subjects (such as reading, writing, math, science, history)?
- Are solid, objective methods used to instruct my children?
- What textbooks and materials are used?
- What kinds of testing instruments are used?
- How can I be involved in a workable way in making decisions at my children's school?

[Ms. Page continues with a series of questionnaires and checklists. Below are selected questionnaires on topics that will guide you more deeply into the learning culture of your children's school(s).]

How Involved Am I as a Parent?

We often forget that what we do as adults greatly affects our children's achievement. Here's a checklist to fill out on yourself.

- ❑ Am I creating in my child a love for learning?
- ❑ Do I see that my children do their homework every night?
- ❑ Do I make sure their homework is appropriate in content and amount?
- ❑ Do I send a note explaining an absence on the day my children return to school?
- ❑ Have I met my children's teacher?
- ❑ Do I know my children's teachers' educational objectives?
- ❑ Do I communicate well and often with my children's teacher(s)?
- ❑ Do I know what my children's assignments are?
- ❑ Do I send my children off to school with a nutritional breakfast?
- ❑ Am I teaching my children the value of being responsible for school work by being responsible for my own work?
- ❑ Do I return all necessary forms on time?
- ❑ Do I avoid making my children tardy or absent?
- ❑ Do I teach my children respect for the school, teacher, and classmates?
- ❑ Do I supply my children with necessary school supplies?
- ❑ Did I attend parent information meetings (e.g., back-to-school nights, open houses)?
- ❑ Do I attend at least two parent-teacher conferences a year?

Am I knowledgeable about:

- ❑ the knowledge and skills my children are being taught?
- ❑ the textbooks they're using?
- ❑ the kinds of tests being used and what the results really mean?
- ❑ how I can best help my children learn?

You as a parent are responsible for each of these items. Your involvement can vastly improve your children's academic performance.

How Good Is My Children's School?

Evaluate your responses to the following list of questions.

- ❑ Do your children like to go to school? Why or why not?
- ❑ Are students held accountable for their performance and behavior?
- ❑ Are children being challenged to the highest level of their ability?
- ❑ Do teachers contact parents regularly for positive as well as negative reasons?
- ❑ Are teachers responsive to parents' questions and concerns?
- ❑ Do the teachers clearly communicate the objectives and standards in core academic areas such as reading, English, math, history, and science?
- ❑ Is the bulk of classroom time devoted to core academics as opposed to non-academic areas?
- ❑ Do staff members clearly demonstrate their commitment to teaching?
- ❑ Does the principal demonstrate effective leadership?
- ❑ How well does the principal know each student?
- ❑ Is the principal available to parents?
- ❑ Are parents welcome to make appointments for classroom visits and treated cordially when they visit?
- ❑ Are parents informed of their rights to see their children's records and files?
- ❑ Are parents' phone calls returned courteously and promptly by the teacher or principal?
- ❑ Is the school environment welcoming and cheerful?
- ❑ Are the classrooms and playground safe and clean?
- ❑ Is the discipline policy firm, but fair?
- ❑ Are parents invited to participate in the decision-making process on key school issues?

Your children's school should be safe and responsive to students and parents. It should emphasize core academic education.

How Can Communication Be Improved among Parents, Teachers and Administrators?

To achieve a productive working relationship, parents and school personnel must develop mutual respect. For example, parents with questions should follow the proper chain of command: Go first to the person with whom they have the concern. This saves time, eliminates misunderstandings, and minimizes the perception that parents are trying to be adversarial. Parents should also be sensitive about when the teacher or principal can meet with the parent. Many parents are not aware that they delay or interrupt instruction for all students when they try to talk to the teacher during an unscheduled meeting at the beginning of class. Interrupting school personnel, especially during recess or lunch time, can cause them to avoid supervising students as they should.

Scheduling a time outside of the school day can make a difference in whether the parent is barely heard or listened to with understanding. With a little giving on both sides, many of these difficulties can be overcome.

Parents should ask themselves the following questions:

- Do I consider the scheduling constraints of the teachers and the principal when I ask to talk with them about my concerns?
- Do I choose a time that is good for them as well as for me?
- Do I show the teacher and principal respect and courtesy, realizing that the way I treat them signals how I want them to treat me? (Have I practiced the Golden Rule?)
- When I meet with school personnel, do I acknowledge that they also care about my children and have a lot invested in them?
- Do I ask specific well-thought-out questions so I can be given a clear response?
- Do I ask teachers what they need from me so they can work more effectively with my children?

Both parents and educators have an obligation to do their part in building a positive relationship. Just as the line from Mary Poppins says, "A spoonful of sugar makes the medicine go down," a little courtesy and thoughtfulness can help you deal with difficult issues in the school environment.

What Kind of Communication Should I Receive from the School?

Newsletters. Many school districts mail a newsletter to parents, which contains the dates of important school board meetings and districtwide functions as well as opportunities for you to volunteer. It may also explain key issues before the school board. In addition, the school may have its own newsletter, which should keep you up-to-date on schoolwide activities. Some teachers also send home a classroom newsletter.

Read carefully the newsletters you receive. Many times they contain useful information that will provide checkpoints on curriculum and other school concerns. You may also be able to volunteer to help put one of these newsletters together, which would provide access to other valuable information.

Parent Information Meetings. The school and the school district should schedule several meetings throughout the year, such as an introductory meeting at the beginning of the year. This is called "Back to School Night," or a similar name. Attend this meeting, because it is an excellent opportunity for you to get to know your children's teacher(s) and to find out the academic objectives for the year. Parent-teacher conferences should be scheduled once or twice a year. In addition, schools generally hold an "Open House" in the spring. Don't miss any of these opportunities to gain important information about your children's education program.

If the school does not create opportunities for communication, you should take the initiative yourself. Establish a positive rapport with the teacher and principal as soon as possible. Feel free to ask questions or make an appointment to visit the classroom. You can set the tone for positive communication by your own interaction with the principal and teachers. This helps enormously if a problem arises later. Model the courteous behavior that you would like to have extended to you.

What Are the Roles and Responsibilities of School Personnel?

Productive school-home relations can be achieved through effective communication between parents and school personnel. The questions parents ask in their interaction with the school generally involve the following school personnel.

- The *superintendent* is responsible for the entire district. He or she is not usually aware of individual classroom activities, but works with principals, district office staff, and with the school board instead of individual teachers. *Administrators* work in the school district office, choosing and implementing district policy.

- The *principal* is responsible for all school policies. He or she does not grade students and does not know every classroom detail. Principals or vice-principals generally handle major student disciplinary problems on campus.

- *Teachers* are responsible for all activities in their classrooms. Generally, they are not responsible for setting schoolwide policies. They help students to become successful and assign grades according to the student's performance in class. Teachers generally handle minor disciplinary problems.
- *Counselors* and *school psychologists* have varied roles. Some, particularly in high schools, are largely responsible for career and college guidance. Others do actual counseling, and may be responsible for testing for learning disabilities. Many counselors have some limited disciplinary role, especially if the problem is related to a behavior or learning disorder.
- *School nurses* are responsible for physical health in school. They determine when students are ill and inform the parents. Nurses may have some teaching responsibility for such subjects as health, nutrition, and sex education. They may also keep health records on each student.
- *School secretaries* are responsible for running the school office, and they maintain student records. They don't make decisions on student grades and are not responsible for discipline.
- *Classroom and playground aides/assistants* assist teachers with various duties both in and out of the classroom. Generally, aides report to the teacher to whom they are assigned.
- *Cafeteria workers and custodians* have jobs primarily related to areas of the school requiring their services. Like secretaries, they do not make decisions on student grades or discipline, but many play an important role in the life of the student.

How Can I Try to Change a School Policy with which I Don't Agree?

If you believe that the school needs to be improved in a certain area, try the following.

- Partnering with a committee of parents, present your ideas to the principal, the local school association, and/or the superintendent of schools. Be sure you have a number of parents who support what you would like to do.
- If the principal and local school council support your request, work with them to develop ways to implement it at the school.
- If the local school does not support your request, try to influence the superintendent. If that fails, go directly to the board of education. Ask to be placed on the agenda under "requests to speak" or "oral communication." Have a number of supportive parents attend the meeting when you present your case.

- If the board of education does not respond, discuss your ideas with the local media: newspapers, magazines, and television and radio stations.
- Change may come slowly. Don't give up. Attend board meetings. Keep talking to the media. If conditions are intolerable, take legal action.
- If all else fails, lobby your state legislators for change.

Three Helpful Rules for Getting Your Questions Answered

The most vital component for an effective, cooperative effort between parents, teachers, and administrators in schools is a positive relationship. But good relationships don't just happen. Both educators and parents must make a concerted effort to build positive, trusting relationships through mutual courtesy, respect, and efforts to accommodate without compromising convictions.

The second key area is clear, effective communication. Clear, regular, two-way communication is necessary for parents to remain effectively involved in their children's education. When parents don't understand the school program, they worry about what is really going on at school. When educators don't take the time to listen with empathy to parents' questions and comments (without feeling threatened and without judging them), communication is hindered. It is both the parents' obligation and the school's obligation to do their part to ensure that this happens. Often, effective communication can diffuse a problem before it starts.

The third important rule is one that we all know—The Golden Rule. If parents, teachers, and administrators treated each other as they would like to be treated in the same circumstances, it would change the face of public education today. If teachers and administrators listened and responded to every question asked by a parent with sensitivity and concern, it would have an extremely powerful effect toward building the relationship that is so important. If teachers and administrators were treated with the respect and courtesy their dedication to the students deserves, it would also help to establish a firm foundation for working together productively and for resolving differences. "Do unto others as you would have them do unto you" still works if we apply it.

MORE FAMILY RESOURCES FROM
Broadman & Holman

OUR COUNTRY'S FOUNDERS
William J. Bennett

Written in the same format as *Our Sacred Honor*, *Our Country's Founders* educates young readers on how the founders of our nation felt about, dealt with, and struggled over a variety of issues. Award-winning author William Bennett offers poignant introductions to each chapter. A book that teens will enjoying turning to and parents will enjoy giving. 0-8054-1600-5 *Available 9/98*

READY, SET, READ
Barbara Curtis

Basic reading skills have declined steadily among America's children over the past twenty years, and it's up to parents to nurture and encourage children in their reading abilities. Written by a woman who proved these techniques on her own eleven children, this book is a simple, thorough, and very affordable tool that shows parents how to develop a love of reading in their preschool children.
0-8054-0167-9

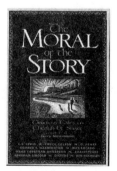

THE MORAL OF THE STORY
Jerry Newcomb, Editor

Inspired by renewed interest in classic stories of virtue, this collection by the world's greatest authors reminds us that exciting, entertaining, inspiring stories can also support traditional Christian moral values. Each of the selections begins with a statement of the moral message, and a suggestion on its suitability for young children. The range of subjects and writing styles makes this book a treasury of great literature for every audience. 0-8054-6199-X

Available at fine bookstores everywhere